More prais
Lifesaving for beginners

In this stunningly eloquent memoir, Edelstein grieves for her mother's drowning to unearth an even deeper grief—the one for her brother who killed himself fifteen years before. In what can be the sometimes garrote of family (as well as its absolute joys) alongside a legacy of mental illness, *Lifesaving for Beginners* is a graceful GPS for finding your safe shore, no matter how distant it seems."
—CAROLINE LEAVITT,
New York Times bestselling author of *Pictures of You* and *Cruel Beautiful World*

Loss, grief, and 'the proof of love' are at stake in this poignant and penetrating memoir of a daughter's quest to understand her elusive mother, the suicide of her beloved brother, and the mystery at the heart of the will to live."
—JILL BIALOSKY,
author of *History of a Suicide: My Sister's Unfinished life*

As if in the eye of a hurricane, Anne Edelstein writes courageously about the deaths that swirl about her. Calm, clear, moving and oh-so poignant, *Lifesaving for Beginners* is a breathtaking portrait of our fruitless efforts to shield each other from the most painful aspects of life. Her book points in another direction and it is indeed a lifesaver."
—MARK EPSTEIN,
author of *The Trauma of Everyday Life* and *Going to Pieces without Falling Apart*

"Anne Edelstein's remarkable debut is an unforgettable—and unputdownable—portrait of a singular American family. Reminiscent of Vivian Gornick's *Fierce Attachments* and Daphne Merkin's *This Close to Happy*, this powerful memoir reads like a conversation with your kindest, funniest, most incisive friend."

—JOANNA RAKOFF,
author of *My Salinger Year* and *A Fortunate Age*

"Anne Edelstein maps the tragic legacy of her brother's suicide and her mother's accidental death with grace and fortitude, shedding light on the darkest of secrets. In the quotidian domain of family life, she finds the simple poetry of love and forgiveness. *Lifesaving for Beginners* is a soaring tribute to the ties that bind us, what makes us whole as human beings."

—ANNE LANDSMAN,
author of *The Devil's Chimney* and *The Rowing Lesson*

Lifesaving for Beginners

a memoir by

ANNE EDELSTEIN

 Red Hen Press | *Pasadena, CA*

Gemini" [excerpt 6.1] from *The First Four Books of Poems*. Copyright © 1968,
1971, 1972, 1973, 1974, 1975, 1976, 1977, 1978, 1979, 1980, 1985, 1995 by Louise Glück.
Reprinted by permission of HarperCollins Publishers.

Rose in the Garden" copyright © Karla Bonoff. Reprinted by permission of
Karla Bonoff. All rights reserved.

Note: Some names and certain identifying characteristics have been changed
to protect the privacy of the individuals described.

Book design by Selena Trager

Library of Congress Cataloging-in-Publication Data
Names: Edelstein, Anne author.
Title: Lifesaving for beginners : a memoir / by Anne Edelstein.
Description: First edition. | Pasadena, CA : Red Hen Press, 2017.
Identifiers: LCCN 2017011415 | ISBN 9781597096058 (pbk. : alk. paper) | ISBN
9781597095792 (ebook) Subjects: LCSH: Edelstein, Anne. | Edelstein, Anne—
Family. | Book editors—United States—Biography. | Literary agents—United
States—Biography. Classification: LCC PN149.9.E44 A3 2017 | DDC 818/.603
[B]—dc23 LC record available at https://lccn.loc.gov/2017011415

The National Endowment for the Arts, the Los Angeles County Arts Commission, the Dwight Stuart Youth Fund, the Max Factor Family Foundation,
the Pasadena Tournament of Roses Foundation, the Pasadena Arts & Culture
Commission and the City of Pasadena Cultural Affairs Division, the City of
Los Angeles Department of Cultural Affairs, the Audrey & Sydney Irmas Char-
itable Foundation, Sony Pictures Entertainment, Amazon Literary Partnership,
and the Sherwood Foundation partially support Red Hen Press.

First Edition
Published by Red Hen Press
www.redhen.org

Acknowledgments

My profound gratitude is for my mother, who brought me into this world, for Danny, who was not here long enough, and for all of my family for their love. I thank Andrea Valeria for telling me I would write this book, and the friends who have read it along the way, especially Andrea Chapin, and Becky Saletan, Deb Futter, David Rakoff, Krista Ingebretson, Kathleen Finneran, Sarah Cohen, and Liel Leibovitz. I thank my friend and agent, Gail Hochman, whose wise words and indefatigable spirit allowed this book to be; and I thank Kate Gale and the folks at Red Hen for publishing it! My deepest appreciation goes to Eli and Eva, for their perpetual inspiration and beauty, and beyond all to Roy, who has read more versions of this memoir than anyone, and who is always at my side.

For Eli and Eva

There is a soul in me
It is asking
to be given its body

—Louise Glück, *Gemini*

. . . it is always the same truth: love must wait for wounds to heal. It is
the waiting we must do for each other, not with a sense of mercy, or in
judgment, but as if forgiveness were a rendezvous.

—Anne Michaels, *The Winter Vault*

August 2000

The Lily Pond is almost too large to qualify as a pond, nearly a mile-long swim all the way to the other side and back. Today is as perfect as it gets, the sun sparkling on the tiny waves of current. I am smiling and relaxed as I reach my long-swim destination of the big yellow rock. I feel so lucky to be in this beautiful place in Maine, so isolated and so human, so far away from the everyday world of the other eleven months of the year.

There can be challenges in the pond. And there's definitely a tinge of the preciousness of life, if not actual danger, out there swimming alone with nothing but the beauty of the water, the sky and the rocks and trees surrounding you. This summer someone told me that there was some bad garbage dumped at the pond's far edge. There *is* something about that end of the pond that's eerie. When I heard the tale about the bad garbage, even though I never did find out exactly what that was, I was a little relieved never to have actually touched the other bank. But we've been coming here for four summers now, and each year the distance of my swim reaches closer to the far end of the pond.

Sometimes on the way back, the surface gets surprisingly choppy, to the point that I realize how strong my body needs to be to swim through the current. Every once in a while two swimmers pass each other in the water. Once, a teenage boy actually asked me if I wanted to race.

One day last week, about halfway through my swim to the yellow rock, there was a huge bird perched up high in a tree. It looked like a hawk, but with the long beak of a heron. It *really* looked like a hawk when it spread its wings and flew across the pond above me. I kept on swimming, telling myself that I knew that birds didn't attack people. And then it flew back over me again, returning to its original perch. As I envisioned my birds-eye mass of dark, curly hair bobbing up and down in the water, I found myself frantically doing the dog paddle, undecidedly lurching from one direction to the other, trying to figure out which way to go. I finally got my bearings and decided to turn back, still reluctant about shifting course partway through. With the image of my children playing happily on the shore firmly pressed into my mind, I swam as quickly as I could.

One

The phone rings in what must be the middle of the night. When I look at the clock, it's actually only a few minutes before midnight. It's not the usual screech of a fax machine mistakenly dialed to our phone line, or the slurred voice of an occasional wrong number. It's my brother at the other end of the line. I'm strangely unconcerned when I hear his voice, even though I know that middle-of-the-night phone calls from family members can be a bad sign. Ted is calling to say that our mother is dead.

"That's impossible," I say. "They're on vacation in Australia." Or were they still in New Zealand? "They've only been away for four weeks. They still have another week before they come home." My mother is only sixty-eight years old. She's always been "healthy as an ox," an unstoppable force.

But sure enough as I look out at the silhouettes of the other apartment buildings against the dark sky, a few lights still turned on in the building behind ours, I'm talking to Ted about my mother's death. It's impossible, but it's true. Just like that, my mother's life has ended, and Ted and I are having the fateful conversation I've been destined to have at some point in my life. But it's nothing at all like what I imagined for my mother's death. What Ted is saying is not right. And the timing is wrong.

"She drowned," Ted is telling me. "They were snorkeling in the Great Barrier Reef, and she drowned." He keeps on talking and I see a picture of my mother in a state of panic, gasping for air. I can't take it in.

I watch my husband Roy watching me, as I hold the receiver in my hand, sitting upright at the edge of our bed. Eva is now crying in her crib because we've decided again to try the experiment of letting her go back to sleep on her own. Eli, who has run into our room to escape the noise of the crying, has already fallen back to sleep in a mound between Roy and me.

I try to take charge by writing down the long Australian phone numbers Ted is reeling off. It's already 5:00 p.m. the next day in Australia, he's saying. Will the official date of her death be March 2, 1998, which is today's date? Or will it be March 3rd, like it is in Australia? Ted reminds me that because it's already late afternoon there, people are leaving their offices. He gives me the home number of the social worker, along with her office number in the hospital. There's also the phone of the local police station, the boating company that took them out into the reef, and the hotel where my parents are staying. I double-check all of the phone numbers with Ted, and then because there's really nothing else we can come up with to say, we hang up.

I tell Roy what I've just heard, the news Ted has just heard from my father, words that sound completely unreal. They were snorkeling. My father was out further. He kept on coming back to find my mother, who was snorkeling closer in, toward the boat, where the water was more shallow. By the time my father found her, she'd already been pulled to shore. Roy nods back at me, like he's trying to give some validity to what I'm saying.

I try dialing some of the different phone numbers on the list, but can't get through. Finally I connect with my father at the police station in Cairns, the town next to the Great Barrier Reef. He says he's waiting to get the results of the autopsy report from the police. They'd been snorkeling under the auspices of a boating company, so an official autopsy is required, he tells me. Besides, the body can't be released from the country without an autopsy. "We specifically chose this boat company because it was safe," my father says. "The boat left from a sandy beach. Your mother was wearing a life jacket. She wasn't out deep. There were other people there, too, from our group."

My father tells me he'd snorkeled back and forth four times, looking for my mother, to bring her out to where he was, where the fish were more beautiful, but he couldn't find her. The last time a man from the group swam over to him to ask whether he was looking for a woman with gray hair. By the time my father made it to my mother's side on the beach, they couldn't resuscitate her.

I tell my father that Ted and I will fly to Australia to meet him. "No, I want to come back on my own." He's firm on this. "That would hold me up another thirty-six hours if you came. I want to get home." He's already spoken to a travel agent, and it's been arranged. He says he'll settle things at the police station, go back to the hotel for his bags, and get on the very long flight back to Boston the next morning. And he won't take the Valium they've given him. He wants my mother to be in his thoughts like she's supposed to be. They had a magnificent trip, he tells me. They held hands the day before when they walked down the streets of Cairns. His voice sounds dreamy, like they were in love, like it was some kind of second honeymoon, which is almost as otherworldly as the fact that my mother has just died in the Great Barrier Reef.

I wonder about whether to call my uncle Nate to tell him right away, or if I should wait until morning. The news about my mother is strange, but my family is used to death. Unbelievably, Nate is now the only one of my mother's siblings who is still alive. My aunt Cecile died only a year and a half ago from a quick-spreading cancer, my uncle Joe eight years before that when he committed suicide, and now my mother in this mysterious drowning. They've all died younger than they were supposed to, my mother the oldest in life and now in death at age sixty-eight. And then there's the death that has always been the hardest, my brother Danny who was only twenty-two when he died. Shocked as I am about my mother, I see no need to act rashly. It's 2:00 a.m. so I decide I might as well give Nate the rest of the night's sleep before calling him to say what's happened.

I just lie there flat on my back, solitary, Roy having drifted back to sleep. I stare up at the ceiling, trying as hard as I can to imagine it—the figure of my mother in the beautiful, blue sea under a big, bright sky.

At 5:30 a.m. when I hear Eva's cry, I take her to the other side of the apartment where we can be quiet and alone. Together on the living room couch, her body falls back to sleep on top of me. The early sun begins to light up the room. I look out at the Hudson River, wide and gray and almost stagnant this morning. My mother is now dead, I tell myself.

Eva, very much alive, sleeps peacefully on my chest, her warm breathing delicious. For a few moments it makes sense, there's an order to this picture. My mother, with her plush body that once gave birth to me, is on one end. Eva, a year-and-a-half-old perfect bundle of life, is at the other. And I'm in between. But then the logic is lost. My mother, whose life has forever been entangled with mine, has just drowned on the other side of the world.

Danny, the closest touch I've had to death until now, was six years younger than me. He committed suicide when he was only twenty-two in what still, fifteen years later, seems like an impossibly painful way, with a knife. There have been other suicides in the family, too. It was five years after Danny died when my uncle Joe sealed off the windows and doors in his apartment and turned on the gas in the oven. Way before that my grandfather took a lot of pills and died in the men's baths on the Lower East Side, but that happened before I could remember, when I was only a newborn baby, and I didn't even know about it until I was twenty-five. My uncle Joe used to say that our family had a "history of violence." But even after living through Danny's death, I didn't really understand what he meant. Maybe I was just used to it, so I didn't see the point of giving it a label.

It's already clear that my mother's death is completely different from Danny's, and it's not only because it's my mother. For one thing, my mother never would have chosen to die. She hated suicide. When Danny died, she refused to talk about it, for fear that people would pity her, she said. Even

8 | *Lifesaving for Beginners*

outside the family, when the husband of one of her closest friends attempted suicide a few years ago, she was angry, not sympathetic in the least. With Danny's death there had been the intense pain of it, not only what must have been his own unbearable pain but the pain we all had to live with afterwards. And there had been the ongoing spookiness behind his decision, the unyielding quest for answers that could never be known. My mother died in the ocean, with fish all around her. Maybe that's what makes it seem so impossible, that it might have been peaceful and that it happened halfway around the world.

It's a good sign that my mother died at the beach, I reason. I know how much she loved the beach. And if there was one place where my mother and I ever managed to unite, it was by the ocean. We'd had a lifetime of struggle between us—of me trying to get her to understand who I was, of her not listening, of me never wanting to be anything like her, but still wanting to know for sure that she loved me. But our long walks on the beach could be soothing—the texture of the sand, sometimes hot and dry, sometimes wet and grainy between our toes, the sound of the water lapping up next to us. It was the edge of the ocean that had the power to create a bond between my mother and me, to quiet our differences. I picture it to be beautiful where my mother died, and that gives me a little peace.

My mother retired from her longtime position of Hebrew school principal just before they took their trip to New Zealand and Australia. "I want to leave before people want me to leave," my mother had said repeatedly. "I never want people saying it's time for her to retire." My mother's reputation was crucial to her. I always wished she'd care more about me than about how she appeared to others. But if appearance was what she was after, she was a success. Right up until she died, she was well-known and admired all around Boston for her work in Jewish education. For seventeen years she'd been the principal of a prominent religious school, something she wore as a badge of honor. Ever since I was twelve, my mother taught Hebrew school and she talked about her work incessantly. "My parents," "my teachers," even "my children" was how she referred to the people at her Hebrew school. It would really get on my nerves. "Aren't *we* her children?" my brothers and I would joke. But strangely, now that my mother has died a day ago, I've tipped into a newfound appreciation for her public accomplishments.

It surprises me, but unquestionably I want to say something at my mother's funeral. I know there will be all kinds of rabbis and teachers and mentors speaking about her, and that they will have all kinds of praise for my mother. But it turns out I have plenty to say myself. I begin to plan a speech, and lots of images surface right away. I can distinctly see the sparkle in her eye. There's a kind of strength to her solid constitution that always propelled her and allowed her to accomplish all that she did. It dawns on me that even though she could be unaware of people's feelings, especially mine, as she plowed through life, I respect her. In leafing through the volumes of poetry collections on the shelf, I find the right poem by Louise Glück. It's called "Gemini," coincidentally the same astrological sign as my mother, and it has beautiful images that stir up the way my mother and I are connected. It will be my personal prayer, a way for people to understand that it was my mother who died on the other side of the ocean.

≈

It was only six months ago, what I now know to be just in time before she died, that I began to feel a distinct shift in feeling towards my mother. It was right after I saw the Woody Allen movie, *Deconstructing Harry*. The Woody Allen character wasn't anything like me, and his father wasn't anything like my mother. But after seeing that movie, the wastefulness of a lifetime of antagonism between me and my mother, the only one I would ever have, became inescapable. It was then that I'm sure something changed between us, almost like the flick of a switch.

Not that it made what happened before entirely go away. I could still sometimes get that clenched feeling when I spoke to my mother on the phone, something that would probably never disappear completely. In all of those many years since I'd left home, when I'd talk to my mother every couple of weeks, mechanically reporting on whatever events I could come up with, I had to be careful not to reveal too much. I knew that she could be unpredictable, that sympathy could quickly turn into criticism. Almost from birth, it seemed that we'd never mesh. A therapist once told me there was actually a term for it: "mismatch," and there wasn't anything I could do to change that. I was used to keeping my guard with my mother. But every once in a while I'd still slip and regret it, like the time when I gleefully told her I was pregnant with Eli. "Are you fat yet?" was what she said in response. Not the happiness I was looking for, the excitement about my having a baby, the grandchild she had supposedly been aching for me to have more than anything. There was just that voice of anxiety, with a small insult to go with it. I vowed never to make the same mistake again. I'd never have the mother I hoped for. And I never did mention the ongoing nausea that persisted through most of my pregnancy, or for that matter my excitement when the unborn Eli began doing flips inside of me.

Way before I was pregnant with Eli, I never mentioned to my mother my strong desire to have children, something I'd felt as far back as when I'd played with my dolls. Even back then, I knew to be careful, to keep those feelings to myself about how I would someday be a mother, nothing like my own mother. First of all, I told myself, I'd always try to understand my children. I also instinctively understood that before bringing a new being into the world, I had to know more than just that I wasn't anything like my mother. And as the years passed, I sometimes wondered if I'd ever figure out what that was. Remarkably, life ran its course and turned out as I wished, and I'm now the mother of two magnificent children.

Even though I'm certain that my mother and I turned a corner in those months before she died, we still had a long history dividing us. Growing up, it seemed she would take just about anyone else's side except for mine, even people she barely knew. There was the time in kindergarten when the teacher yelled at me for talking to my best friend and made me cry. I was embarrassed and wanted the teacher to feel really bad, so I took a small piece of red thread from the hem of my dress and put it in the corner of my eye, to make her think her yelling had made my eye turn red. When the teacher called my mother suggesting that maybe there was some trouble at home and that she should consider taking me to a psychiatrist, my mother immediately sided with the teacher, agreeing that I might be seriously defective. It was my grandmother, who happened to be visiting from New York, who came to the rescue. "That teacher's the crazy one!" my grandmother said, getting my mother to give up on the psychiatrist plan. Still, my mother didn't stop leaving me stranded when authorities were involved. When I turned sixteen and was struggling to pass my driver's test, even managing to do a three-point turn on our clunky manual shift car, my mother allied herself with the department of motor vehicles man. "Do you really think it's OK to give her the license?" she asked him. It was "with a heavy heart" that he was willing to let me pass, he said, as my mother nodded in agreement.

And there were all of those times when my mother would scream at me for not being happy. The most outrageous was the Thanksgiving right after Danny died, when we were driving around Washington, my father looking for a parking space, me sitting painfully silent in the back seat. "Why are you so unhappy?" she yelled, her voice sharp and accusatory. Or possibly she even dared to use the word "depressed" over my wretched condition. "Maybe you should get some help!" she berated me. "Or," she grew louder, "some medication!" The fact was that I couldn't have been more miserable. Probably depressed *was* the most accurate description, but how could I not be? I'd just experienced the brutal loss of my brother only a month before, and here we were at our first family reunion afterwards. Didn't it have to be unbearable for her, too?

"When your own kids are born, you'll understand her better," friends would say. But the fact was that when Eli came into the world, my distance from my mother seemed all the more definite, and sadder. The fundamental depth of love I felt for my own child just didn't seem to be in my mother's sphere. I no longer just felt sorry for myself, but I felt sorry for her, too, for all that she must have missed in being a mother.

But in those last months something had stirred in me, maybe in both of us. I came to see what I'd always taken to be my mother's compulsion to undermine, as her own frazzled version of protection, disconnected as it may have been. We had definitely started talking to each other differently on the phone, I was sure of it. That nervousness about imparting some new piece of information had begun to disappear. When I saw her in person, just before they went on their trip to Australia, I was positive something had changed. She and my father came to babysit that weekend as an anniversary gift to Roy and me, so that we could stay in a hotel for a couple of nights on our own. I'd insisted to Roy that we rush back that morning after breakfast, thinking my mother would be tense and ready to leave. But when she greeted us, she was kind and happy. And the kids seemed happy, too. That was the last time we saw each other.

~

This clean white apartment, with its high ceilings and sweeping views of the Hudson, has been my home for five years now. That's almost as long as I've lived anywhere, and it's still remarkable to me. When it comes to real estate, Roy has incredible talent. He doesn't have to think about what makes a life stable, he just knows what a good and comfortable home is and how to find it. My approach is much less expansive. If it were just me, I'd probably still be in some small apartment downtown with a view of nothing much. True, it would be perfectly arranged according to my own taste, pictures hung just right, and the pattern of each fabric carefully selected. I do know from having moved from place to place how to make a new location my own. But it would be nothing at all like this big,

open space with the magnificent view of the river that changes every day depending on the light and the wind. Where we
live is an oasis of a home, still bare and spare because Roy and
I can't always agree on what art to hang or which furniture to
buy, but that's also part of its loveliness. It's taken me a long
time to find the way to this airy, beautiful place that I can re-
liably call my home. I still marvel at the calm I've found here.

Of all our different homes growing up, Marblehead is the
place I loved most. Even if my mother and I had been a rest-
less combination, I'm sure we had an easier time during those
childhood years in Marblehead. It's where I first learned to
swim in the chilly salt water. Every warm day of the summer, we'd go to the beach. It was difficult to keep your balance walking over the big, round stones at the entrance. They
would grind under your feet until the beach smoothed out
into small pebbles and then dark sand where we could take off
our sandals and spread out the beach blanket. My mother was
happy in those summer days, sitting at the edge of the water
and laughing with her friends, Danny next to her on the blanket. Teddy and I would go off to play in the old, broken sewage
pipe, where we could make echoing noises with our voices. It
was at the beach where I made my first best friends. When we
got older, we'd play by ourselves for hours on the big rocks
that led up to the cliffs, climbing into the crevices where the
small pools of water were lined with what looked like red vel-
vet, filled with snails and baby mussels. We would smash the
mussels with rocks, first trying to guess whether they'd be orange or yellow inside, and we'd pull the legs off of the starfish
because we'd heard they'd grow back on their own.

Marblehead didn't last forever, though, and once we moved to Connecticut it was never really the same. We did get used to it, but it was a little boring. I was ten and Teddy was eight, and Danny must have been only four. Before we moved, my parents told us that maybe we'd get to have a swimming pool in our new house, but that never happened. Even from the air in the new neighborhood you could tell we were no-where near the ocean. Instead, we went to swim at the town pool, where there were two diving boards, lots of splashing, and voices screaming and bouncing off the cement. We had to be careful when we ran not to slip on the concrete. A lifeguard was always blowing his whistle. And always there was a kind of buzzing noise from the lawnmowers keeping the grass cut. I remember thinking when we first moved that in Connecticut there were now two types of noise—clean, like drawing a line in the sand with a stick, and a fuzzy kind of noise that played back and forth in your head. Some of the crispness of life was gone. In Connecticut, it took more than an hour to get to the beach, and that was when we didn't get stuck in traffic. Once we finally got to the ocean, the waves were smaller and less salty, and it was crowded with lots of people we didn't know.

When it came to be time to move back to Massachusetts six years later, when my father wanted to change jobs again, I was excited. But as it happened, our new town was Andover, and it was nothing at all like Marblehead. It immediately be-came clear that it was better to be a little bored in Connecticut, than miserable in what had become our next new home. Only a forty minute drive from Marblehead, we couldn't have been further away from what once was. Something my parents hadn't figured out before we moved was that there was a big difference between Andover the prep school and Andover the high school. And the high school was where I was stuck. The big heroes were the football players and cheerleaders, nothing at all like the 1970s high school I already knew, where people cared about anti-war demonstrations and where to buy pot, not the stupid contests about how many six-packs you could guzzle down in a weekend.

And there were hardly any Jews in Andover, at least not compared to the other places we'd lived. One boy in my class actually asked me if Jews had horns. Danny used to close the drapes in the dining room on Friday nights so no one could see when my mother lit the candles.

I cursed my parents for bringing us to this place. It was true that Andover was about twenty minutes closer to my father's job in Lawrence. But a longer drive seemed like a small price to pay for his family's happiness. I never understood why we hadn't just moved back to Marblehead. There was some excuse about our now being well-located for skiing in the White Mountains. But it was as if they were only confirming their bad decision. Skiing was cold, just like the rest of life. We'd have to wake up at some ridiculously early hour to drive for two hours, only to wait in line for the chair lift in the freezing temperatures. I was never sure of whether my father noticed his obvious mistake, but I was positive that my mother had been much happier in Marblehead. But she'd never admit that. She willed us to be satisfied in what was now our new claustrophobic home, where all we had was each other.

I felt the worst for Danny. Teddy and I didn't have that many years to survive in Andover before we went to college, and we managed to get into Boston on the Peter Pan Bus that thankfully stopped right at the corner of our street. But Dan-

ny was only ten when we moved there. I wished he hadn't had
to spend so many years in that town.

Danny was much more creative about dealing with life in
Andover than I could ever be. For a while, he took to wearing
a ski mask when he rode his bike to school, so he could avoid
the town bullies. With his never-ending sense of humor, he
could always find the joke in a situation. "Curb your laugh,"
he'd say to me, getting me into a hysterical fit of laughter just
as I was trying to kick him out of my room, or yell at him for
bothering me while I was talking on the phone. "You'll laugh
at anything," he'd say. And he was right, I'd laugh at just about
anything that Danny said.

He managed to be elected president of the high school,
and was voted "Most Likely to Succeed" by the senior class,
quite an accomplishment in a town that didn't exactly stand
for individuality. I can still remember his graduation address.
Sitting on the bleachers in the gym, we all heard Danny say
how lucky he and his classmates were to finally be released
from the prison of the high school. I knew by getting out of
prison, he also meant getting out of the town of Andover itself.
For this he received a burst of applause. Danny had even convinced Jay Leno (incredibly enough, he was also an Andover
High grad) to come to speak at the graduation. True, Jay Leno
was not yet at the height of his fame, but still he'd responded
to Danny's invitation.

It was only four years later when the *Andover Townsman*
ran its article, euphemistically saying that Danny had "died
of unnatural causes." None of his high school classmates or
their parents could believe it. That was part of Danny's trick,
he could fool people. I'd known, though, for at least a few
years that he was on a destructive course. When I was half-

way across the country in graduate school and Danny called to tell me about his first acid trip, he was absolutely ecstatic and couldn't wait for the next time. But then he got unnerved about never again achieving that same state of bliss no matter how hard he tried, and I started to get worried. As the years went by, he got more desperate, and would sometimes call to say how frightened he was of his own violence. Once he told me he'd broken all the windows in the house that he shared with friends in college.

You can't really blame a town for someone's death. But I've always thought of Andover as a lifeless place. It's hard to believe that my parents have now lived in that town for thirty years.

≈

Now that it's morning, I call Nate to tell him. Ted had already received the autopsy results from my father, I relay to Nate. No sign of brain damage or heart attack. And the arteries were clean." He silently listens to the facts. "She was wearing a life jacket. She wasn't out far," I tell him. Being a psychiatrist, Nate shifts into a medical role. "It couldn't have been a typical drowning," he says. "If people were around they would have noticed her thrashing." He reasons that it might have been some sort of arrhythmia, something electrical in her heart that wouldn't show up in an autopsy. From what Nate says, it sounds like it must have been sudden, and not painful. I hold onto that. I want to know that it wasn't painful.

I trust Nate. He's twelve years younger than my mother, right in between the generations. He's always been a wonderful uncle. Back when I was only five or six, and Ted was three or four, Nate would come to visit us in Marblehead and we'd play a game called "Uncle Nate" in the backyard. He'd lie down in a lawn chair pretending to be asleep and we'd run around the chair, shouting, "Uncle Nate, Uncle Nate," as loudly as we could until he'd jump up and grab one of us, and we'd shriek with laughter. Sometimes other kids in the close-knit neighborhood of our small, dead-end street would join in, too. And when the sad day would inevitably come when Nate had to go back home, we'd play the game ourselves, taking turns at being Uncle Nate.

In the late '80s, at a point when I could no longer stand the relentless pace of life in New York, I decided to move to Washington, DC, which was where Nate lived. So did my uncle Joe's family, although Joe had already died by then. I didn't really know much about Washington, DC, but it felt like a familiar place because of the many Thanksgivings we'd spent there. And moving was something that came easily to me. I'd been working as a fledgling literary agent and when I got a job offer in Washington, desperate to get out of New York, I took it. Not thinking twice that Washington wasn't a likely place for a career in the publishing business, I packed up all my belongings into a truck and moved there.

If it hadn't been for Nate, I doubt I would have lasted the full two years that I spent in DC. It was clear from the start that the job wasn't going to work out. The boss and I didn't get along, and after six weeks we agreed it made sense to part ways. I patched together a living of freelance editing jobs, ghostwriting, and even typing, until it became obvious that I should set up my own business. That's when I began my own literary agency—editing the book proposals and the manuscripts of my new clients and selling their work to publishers—and eventually, of course, I moved back to New York.

Those two years that I braved Washington, I was pretty estranged, and could easily fade into the internal world of my apartment, which had also become my office. But something kept me from moving back to New York right away. When it wasn't too languid, Washington could be a pleasant place. The slower pace made life easier. And I discovered that through the act of swimming I could get myself circulating in the outside world. Unlike anything I would have ever dreamt possible in New York, in DC during the long summer season I could just walk right into almost any local hotel swimming pool and pretend I belonged there. I'd spread out my towel on a lounge chair, jump into the pool, which was usually empty, and swim laps. Partly, I was inspired by having recently seen the movie of *The Unbearable Lightness of Being*, where Juliette Binoche swims in a clear, turquoise pool, a beautiful sight to behold. I imagined that maybe I could be like her, doing the breaststroke, back and forth, losing myself in the strokes and the motion of the water. I'd come out feeling refreshed and alert, limbs strong. I'd bring along a manuscript or a book, and read it at the poolside before jumping in for more laps. The water was a refuge.

≈

Eli watches as I pack, his big, brown eyes staring straight at me when I look up from my suitcase. "Where are you going?" he asks.

"To visit Papa Joel, remember?"

Eli, who's just turned four two months ago, has already been trying to figure out what death could possibly mean, even before I told him the news about my mother. "George

Washington must have been very lonely when he was a little boy," he had reasoned to me only last week. "What do you mean?" I'd asked. "Because when he was alive, no one was born yet," he explained logically. His grandmother's death would be a new piece in his puzzle.

This morning when I told Eli that Grandma Lois had died, I tried to be as careful as possible. If there was one thing I thought I knew about dealing with death, it was that it was important to be honest with your children. But Eli's brain was just now beginning to process what the huge notion of death could possibly mean, and I needed to tread lightly. I knew to steer away from the fact that she died in the water, especially with Eli, who was already a little uneasy about swimming. There was a stage when he was one-and-a-half until he was two, when I couldn't even convince him to get in the bathtub. Before talking to Eli, I'd consulted with a friend who's a child psychologist. He'd agreed it was wise not to mention the water, and also said I should try to avoid the word "accident" or even saying that my parents had been on vacation when my mother died. "Make sure you tell him that your father was with your mother when it happened," he'd advised. "And stress that your father is still alive. That's very important." I tried to plan out exactly what I would say ahead of time. I'd concentrate on Grandma Lois's age. "She was old," I would say, very old. And her body stopped working because it was old."

I decided it was the right moment when Eli and I were on our way to the Bank Street Bookstore around the corner, to buy a birthday present for his friend. Together we pushed open the heavy wrought iron front doors of our building. Something very sad happened," I began. "Papa Joel called to say that Grandma Lois died. Papa Joel doesn't really know what happened," I recited. "It had something to do with her health, and that she was old. *I'm not* old," I knew to say. "I'm going to go to visit Papa Joel, to help make him feel better and try to find out more about what happened. Then we'll all go up to visit Papa Joel together."

Eli listened to my speech, his eyes wide. "I'm young, right?" asked Eli, who was very proud to be four.

"Yes, right, you're very young."

"But I get older and bigger every day, right?"

"Yes, you do."

"And I get to be a better and better fighter." Thankfully, he was changing the topic.

"You do. And next year you'll go to kindergarten and you'll learn to read," I chimed in. That was it. We continued on our way to the bookstore to buy his friend a present.

That was this morning, and until now we haven't mentioned my mother again. I'm trying to figure out what I need to put in my suitcase before I start making dinner. Tomorrow I'll need to get up early to take the first shuttle up to Boston. Ted will drive up tonight from Connecticut to meet my father's plane when he arrives from Australia. The plan is for the both of them to meet me at the airport in the morning, and then the three of us will drive up to Andover to take my father home.

"You're sad because your mom died, right?" Eli asks. His face is looking right at me. His voice sounds wise, like he wants to know something else. But I don't know what more I can tell him, so I don't say anything. I dig into the back of the bottom drawer and find an old flannel nightgown, because I figure it will be cold in my parents' house. Before closing the suitcase, I give Eli a hug, and hope that will be enough for now.

I can see the figures of my father and brother behind the glass panel in the "arrivals" area at Logan Airport. They strike me as a meager greeting party, standing there by themselves in the near distance. Even though I know that my mother's body, no longer alive, is still in Australia and Danny has now been dead for fifteen years, there's still the feeling that we're supposed to be a family of five. As I get closer, I can see that my father is tanned after spending a month in New Zealand and Australia, where it's been summer. Ted looks pale, even though he's naturally darker and taller than my father, and he's bent over him protectively. It's a lonely feeling seeing just the two of them. They see me, too, and we find our way to each other. We embrace for a long time, at last joined together on this strange odyssey.

My father sits in the back seat of Ted's new Subaru station wagon. I see him kick an old candy wrapper on the car floor, with what seems to be annoyance. Ted may drive a station wagon like we did growing up, but his car is sloppy with old papers, half-eaten packages of candy, and kids' toys. My father always kept the seats and floors of our rusty old Ford Falcon vacuumed clean. "I had to leave your mother behind. I couldn't stay any longer," he apologizes. "There were still more papers to be filed before they'd release her. It should only be a couple more days until she's back." He talks about my mother's body like she's still alive. Ted and I nod back at him. We already know that my father hadn't been able to get the autopsy report to the right authorities before leaving, that he had to leave the official procedures in the hands of the police. Once all the red tape was complete, her body could be flown from Cairns to Melbourne and then finally released from Australia. It would be at least another few days before my mother's body would be home.

"I had to leave her," he says again.

"I don't think we can have the funeral until the body arrives," Ted says. "They'll tell us more when we get to the funeral home." Our appointment at Levine Chapels is scheduled for eleven, he tells us. It only now occurs to me that there's an itinerary for today. And that Ted's already taken care of it. "After Levine Chapels, we'll drive up to Andover to meet with the rabbi," he says. As the middle child he falls naturally into the role of keeping things balanced. His diligence provides a sense of comfort, and is also something that would please my mother.

Although Ted now lives in Connecticut, he still seems well-versed in the streets of Brookline from when my mother's travels took us there regularly. We pass the Judaica store, where she bought Chanukah candles and gifts, and the Jewish delicatessen. He pulls into the parking lot in front of Levine Chapels.

Growing up I had more success than I do now getting Ted to be on my side against my mother. He even used to call her a "yay, rah, rah Jew." We would joke that my mother's dream professions for us were for me to be a Hebrew school teacher, and for Teddy to teach singing. My mother was always quoting the wisdom of the Hebrew school singing teacher, who in her mind was always handsome and charismatic. In the end, though, Teddy made my mother very happy by deciding to become a doctor, and when he was appointed to a position in a hospital outside of New Haven, he even moved back to a suburb not far from where we once lived. Ted hated the way my mother and I would constantly fight. There was no way I could ever act like Ted could, as if everything in our family were just fine, something that my mother tried to observe as intently as she followed religious tradition.

The personnel at Levine Chapels talk to us in hushed tones. They tell us they knew my mother, because of her work at the Hebrew school, and they seem impressed by her. They recommend that we contact the US Consulate in Australia to help speed up the return of her body. Or maybe we could try to get some help from the United Jewish Appeal. They tell us that we should act quickly. Even though it's only Wednesday today, tomorrow will be Friday in Australia and after that it will be too late to get the body back until well into next week. When the body isn't buried a couple of days after the death, you are not going strictly by Jewish law," the funeral director reminds us. Of course we know this already. Even my mother would have probably given up on the ritual given the circumstances, but still we nod back in agreement. "It's really important to have the funeral this weekend, if we possibly can," Ted says, representing the three of us. Maybe this is what people do when someone dies, speculate about the possibility of getting something to happen even if it's impossible.

In Andover, the house looks dilapidated and sad. It's gray and rainy outside, and it's as if the house is actually sinking into the wet slope of the front lawn. The white, painted shingles are ridged with dirt. The faded blue shutters are disheveled, maybe from a winter storm. It looks as if the place has been left empty for a lot longer than a month.

On the outside doormat sits a neat, damp bundle of local newspapers. The newspapers were cancelled when my parents were away, but evidently a neighbor had attended to gathering up the most recent copies of the Lawrence *Eagle-Tribune*, thinking my father might want to see them when he returned. "Retirement Fantasy Trip Turns Into Nightmare," the headlines blare, a large grainy picture of my mother's face on the center of the front page. My mother has become a subject that warrants a sensationalist headline, something I never would have imagined. My father shakes his head and puts the package of newspapers under his arm.

When my father opens the door to the mudroom, the rabbi is already sitting on the bench waiting for us. I've never met this rabbi before, but apparently he joined my parents' congregation a few years ago now, and they know him fairly well. He looks friendly, and younger than I expected.

I flash back to when I entered this same house just after Danny died. There was a different rabbi then, the one we knew and disliked from the years when we all lived here. When he referred to Danny as "a suicide," I was furious and wanted nothing of his attempt at consolation. Ted and I had been desperate to see Danny's body, wanting some kind of proof of the terror of his death, and the rabbi had the audacity to say that to look at our brother's body once it was in its coffin would be to violate Jewish law.

When we did finally see Danny's body it was cold and a little rubbery to the touch, and in fact it did little to validate reality. There Danny was, his twenty-two-year-old self lying perfectly still, eyes closed. He was dressed in a gray wool suit, which made him look like he was in a masquerade costume, playing one last joke. All signs of the wounds he'd inflicted on himself were invisible. Lying head to toe in his coffin, he was a full six feet tall, which was also still hard to believe. He'd always been my younger brother, six years younger. The suit was the same one he'd had on when the three of us had gone to a formal New Year's Eve party a couple of years before. For the party, he'd also worn an old air force hat with a strap under the chin, making fun of the formality of the scene. Lying in his coffin, his pale skin looked a little whiter than it was supposed to be. His freckles were still visible, but already fading. His chestnut hair was still thick. Danny had once drawn a picture of my father with three red horns on his head. When his nursery school teacher had been curious about the meaning, we all laughed, knowing the story of how my father once had hair such a deep red color that his old friends still called him Red," as a nickname. At the time of Danny's crayon drawing, my father still had three remaining clumps of hair, then dark brown, although now all that remains on his bald head is a thin rim of white.

Ted, my father, and I, and the new rabbi huddle around the kitchen table in front of what my mother referred to as the picture window," the cold air now coming in through the panes. I consider going to find the electric space heater. I usually keep it plugged in by my side when I visit my parents during the winter, when the house is always under-heated. But I can't manage to pull myself away from the table. The relatively new wooden floor makes the kitchen slightly warmer than it used to be when it was covered in linoleum.

This house has always been the least attractive of our family homes. It was built in the mid-'60s and never seemed very well constructed. The houses in Marblehead and Connecticut had been colonials, too, but older and more solid. This one looks more like a fake replica of a New England colonial. The house in Marblehead had a sunroom, a room enclosed entirely by windows that was full of light. There was a maple tree in the backyard, and everyone in the neighborhood used to stand in line to climb it. The Connecticut house was more formal, a "center entrance colonial," as my mother called it, on the corner of a street lined with old elms. My mother loved the rows of pink and white peonies that lined the driveway. I remember her saying they were full and mature because they'd been planted a long time ago. The neighborhood in Andover is more of a development, built on what used to be an apple orchard, stripped bare of its trees to make room for the houses. During my last year of high school, the top floor caught on fire due to a faulty wire, and for a few weeks I thought we might be able to move somewhere else. We did get to live in a local hotel for a month while some of the unhealthy fumes aired out. But then we moved back in.

For my mother it had been an ongoing project, trying to improve the house. A few years ago she'd replaced the old blue carpets with area rugs in the dining room and living room, although the upstairs was still covered with that same old blue carpeting filled with years of invisible dust and cleaning products. Sometime during the '80s, when a friend of hers got divorced and became an interior designer, she'd redecorated the living room. They'd found two new sofas covered in orange and blue brocade fabric that went well with the blue of the old carpeting. My mother particularly liked the dark blue parsons table that's behind the sofa. She said she was happy to put the old brown furniture in the basement. My parents had bought those nubby brown couches and chairs when they were first married. My mother told me that she had cried when that furniture first arrived because it didn't look anything like what she'd ordered and then she was stuck with it. Each spring she would cover the couches with slipcovers in a cheerful Paul Klee-type design to make the place look brighter, until it got to be fall and winter again and we went back to the couches being brown.

At some point a few years ago my mother had added some new touches of the past. On the parsons table there are now two old family photos that had been unearthed by my aunt Cecile, who then distributed copies to all the siblings. One is a formal portrait of my mother's grandmother and grandfather, with their four children sitting in front, wearing sailor outfits, the two girls with big, white bows in their hair. The oldest child is Anna, my mother's mother, my grandmother who died before I was born and for whom I was named. Unlike anyone else in the family she had light hair and blue eyes. The other photograph is of Anna as a young woman standing next to her dark, handsome husband Abraham, the grandfather I'd also never known. They're squinting because the sun is in their eyes. Even though my mother proudly displayed the photograph of my grandparents, she almost never talked about them. It was up to me to try to imagine their lives.

I notice that the rabbi must be only a few years older than Ted and me. He seems congenial for a rabbi, and genuinely interested to know how our family worked. He tells us that his role at the funeral will be to talk about my mother's personal life, who she was to her family. There will be two other rabbis participating in the funeral, too, and they will speak about my mother's professional accomplishments. Ted and I each want to say something, I tell the rabbi. And he notes down that he will speak first, then the other two rabbis, then me, and then Ted. In a comment that seems to come from nowhere, the rabbi suggests that maybe my mother for all of her efficiency and capability as a Jewish educator, might have been an anxious mother. "It seems like she worried a lot," he says. "Like she could possibly be a little stifling as a mother." I wonder if he's trying to prompt us. Maybe my mother was more transparent than I realized.

"Yes, she could sometimes let her fearfulness get in the way of our need to explore on our own," I say, happy to supply this information.

"She was a good mother," Ted quickly jumps in. "She was always there for us." Ted would have no critical words, especially now that my mother was no longer here. I don't bother to argue, even though it's always been my reflex. Things are different now. There's no longer a reason to prove anything about my mother.

My father, who has been silent, reaches into the crumpled brown bag by his side and holds out a glossy tourist photo of the two of them. It's as if he's been waiting for this moment to show it to us. He places the picture in the center of the table. There they are, standing on the stairs of the ship, about to go out into the Great Barrier Reef. The name of the boating company, "Ocean Spirit Cruises, Cairns, Australia," is printed in large letters at the bottom of the photograph. The fact that my father, always frugal, had actually made this tourist purchase is evidence that they must have really been on vacation. My mother's face is positively beaming. "Look how happy she is," my father says, his own face coming to life when he talks about my mother.

She really *does* look happy, and relaxed. I scrutinize the picture and see the lines around her eyes that make her look a little older than she is in my mind. The fluffy white hair framing her round face makes her appear softer than I remember. I try to recall exactly when she stopped dyeing her hair. I remember the Miss Clairol hair dye kits that she used in the bathroom sink, and how I was the one who had to teach her to put on eyeliner and mascara, not that I was such an expert myself. She's standing straight and wearing her perfectly acceptable, but not overly stylish attire—a white knit shirt and striped, knit cotton shorts, a little loose so as not to clearly show the shape of her body. Her skin is tanned, like my father's, showing their past weeks in the sun. My father stands beside her, still a few inches taller, although clearly no longer the five feet eleven inches he once claimed to be. He has his arm around her, as if to take care of her, a stance that has always annoyed me because my mother resisted all caretaking. My father looks fit, impressive considering he turned seventy-two while they were away. His face is posed in that serious look he has for pictures, lips closed, not showing his teeth. He has on a baseball cap, something he's taken to wearing ever since he became conscious of exposing his bald head to the sun. His sideburns and eyebrows look very white next to his tan skin. They're an attractive, aging couple. It's still possible to imagine how they must have looked when my mother was a shapely twenty-five-year-old, my father youthful with more hair, and more real innocence. I can also envision how the lines on their faces might increase further, and how their bodies might someday dwindle once they grew older. But I'm being romantic. Growing up, they never struck me as being in love, as attractive as I can now see they once might have been. They usually seemed a little at odds with each other, except strangely enough for right now, in this picture.

≈

Ted has gone back to Connecticut, to his family who is waiting for him. He looked a little worried about leaving us behind, but I could tell he was also relieved to be going back to his own territory. Since Ted married Janet his world has become more separate from mine. When they're together, they can seem like they're withholding opinions, supporting each other in their own private world. When I'm with the two of them, I can get the feeling that I'm doing all of the talking. It's funny because growing up I was always the quiet child, afraid to say too much for fear of being criticized by my mother, while it was Teddy who was supposed to be the outgoing one. But somewhere along the way, we seem to have switched roles. Sometimes it still seems like Ted wants whatever I have or what I am, even though he's always been the one who's had my mother's love.

It could appear that we have parallel lives. Ted and Janet have two kids, just like we do. David's a year-and-a-half older than Eli, and Karl is two years older than Eva. But Ted's world and his family is separate from mine. They have a three-story Arts and Crafts style house, which they've painted and artfully decorated to make it really comfortable. Sometimes they talk about moving to another neighborhood that's less urban than where they live on the outskirts of New Haven, but they seem to really belong in their house. Both kids are very shy, and seem most at ease in the language of their own family in their own home. While they warm up to Eli and Eva when we all get together, they don't often speak to me or Roy. Ted and Janet seem to have successfully created a world of their own, a world that they've shaped to be pleasing and safe. Maybe it's a better version of the childhood home my mother tried to create for us.

As I help my father unpack, he keeps on urging me to take some of my mother's clothes for myself, even though they'll never fit me. "She looked so nice in this," he says, sweetly holding out a blouse or a sweater before placing it in my mother's drawer. She had a classic style." I smile at his romanticized view of my mother, whose taste in clothes had waned over many years of living with my father's thriftiness. When I was a child, my mother had been more attentive to her appearance, even vain. I remember her reading me a story about a character who was vain, and I couldn't tell if it was supposed to be a good trait or a bad one. When I went to college, I took her old Persian lamb coat with me. She'd bought it before she married my father, and she had to save up for it with the money from her first job. It was a lovely shade of curly gray, long and sweeping, with big cuffs. It kept me warm through the upstate New York winters, which were even longer and bleaker than the ones in New England. Now I can't remember when I'd left it behind or where.

I remember when my mother bought a beautiful, powder-blue crepe dress to wear to Nate and Nan's wedding, Nan, my new aunt-to-be. It was knee-length, and it had a short train in the back. It was going to be a small wedding, with just the brothers and sisters attending. But then they eloped, and I witnessed my mother's disappointment, that she wouldn't get to see them get married, and that she wouldn't get to wear the dress, and I felt like I'd lost something, too. Over the years, I noticed my mother's taste shift from subtle grays and deep, rich shades of red to bold colors with big designs.

She seemed to have gotten stuck on the style of the '70s, which was still reflected in the wallpaper of my old bedroom— big bright yellow, orange, and green flowers, still shiny. I must have followed my mother's advice when it came to choosing that wallpaper. The bedroom had always been louder than I was, and made me shrink a little. My mother had years ago converted the room into an office for herself, and had lined the shelves with her Jewish textbooks and spiral notebooks, disregarding the setting entirely.

Despite my father's attempts, I don't take any of my mother's clothes, but instead accept a couple of Balinese purchases she had made—a wooden duck and a carved wooden box, and a batik cloth, which might be tokens of her happiness on the trip. There's also a pair of lambswool slippers they bought for Eva in New Zealand, and a book about a penguin for Eli.

I help my father by gathering up a load of laundry. This chore, along with setting the table, has always been mine. Teddy and Danny were in charge of mowing the lawn, and the three of us would argue about who had to shovel the driveway in the winter. "There isn't much," my father explains. They'd just done their laundry a couple of days earlier in Cairns. I untangle my mother's bathing suit, still damp with some re- maining Australian sand intact. Her worn shorts still have the leftover aroma of suntan lotion mixed with the smell of my mother.

Remembrances of the sand and the waves, of endless childhood afternoons at the beach in Marblehead, all well up. There were the hot grimy car trips home from the beach, and those moments of great warmth, baking in the closed car that had been sitting in the parking lot for hours before we rolled down the windows to drive home.

And there were the long beach walks I continued to take with my mother as I got older. We had covered great distance in those walks, sometimes many miles long, the salty air blowing against our faces. Sometimes they had been walks of reconciliation, sometimes idle chatter, but always there was some unspoken sense of covering ground together. I breathe her in deeply, over and over, as many times as I can. I cry into the clothes, knowing that this will be our last human contact. And finally, in an act that seems cruelly inevitable, I pour out the laundry detergent and start the washing machine.

~

I first learned to swim in small increments because the ocean water was very cold. Even jumping over tiny waves at the edge was a feat because the water was so icy when it touched your toes. To learn to blow bubbles, you had to walk in up to your knees, deep enough so your face would touch the water when you bent over, and the cold water would numb your legs so you had to be quick. Finally I learned to put my whole body into the cold, foamy ocean at our local beach. My mother, I could tell, was a little uneasy in the water. Not that she couldn't swim, but she didn't really look like she enjoyed it. There was always something a little too ceremonious about the way she'd snap the strap of her bathing cap under her chin. She'd walk into the water quickly, right up to her thighs, and then just start swimming rapidly, her head awkwardly turning to take in air just like she was supposed to in between strokes. Then she'd get right out of the water, and go straight back to the blanket.

When I was nine or ten, old enough to go to sleepover camp, I got past the "dead man's float" and floating on my back. In the muddy waters of the camp lake, I learned to breathe and swim at the same time, and once I was able to do a dive from one bent knee I passed Advanced Beginners. The lake water may have been warmer than the ocean, but swimming in the lake was not a carefree experience. If you didn't keep moving, the leeches that lived in the lake could attach themselves to you. The counselors called the leeches "water buddies." When they'd get stuck on your legs, the counselors would put dry sand on them to get them off, but sometimes they wouldn't detach easily and you'd have to pull at them and they'd leave some blood.

Over different summers at different camps I managed to progress as a swimmer, until one summer, much to my amazement, I was good enough to become a Senior Lifesaver. I was never really certain that anyone should actually put their life in my hands. I had a lot of endurance, and knew I'd eventually be able to reach the drowning victim, but I wasn't all that sure I'd get there fast enough. And if the victim ever took to thrashing his arms or legs, I doubted I'd have the body strength to keep him in place. Possibly, if the victim were already out of breath when I arrived, I could cross my arm over his chest like I'd been taught, and haul him back to shore. But I hoped I'd never have to test my abilities.

I grew to love swimming, even though I never got to be fast, and I never perfected a real dive, or even how to breathe right when doing the crawl. To swim in the soft Caribbean or Mediterranean waters was a luxurious discovery, and even the cold Atlantic, which is really what I'm the most used to, is distinctly satisfying each time my muscles stretch out at the beginning of a long swim.

I'm alone with my father in the cold house. I won't get to go back to New York until tomorrow, and I miss Eli and Eva, as their bedtime approaches. I call to say goodnight. "Will you sleep next to Papa Joel in his bed tonight?" Eli asks me over the phone. I picture a small stick figure version of myself sleeping next to my father, and smile at the impossible task of a child protecting their parent. Even now, as an adult, there's not much I can actually do to help my father through his shock and grief. But what really gets to me is thinking about how much a parent can actually do to protect a child. I hope my children will never feel that a parent protecting a child is an impossible job. I remember from a young age feeling that when it came to fears and sadness, we were really all just on our own. What I wanted was for my mother to show up and hold me, to dispel my fears, but usually if anyone would try to help it was my father. When I was small and scared because all the stuffed animals in my room would succeed in coming to life at night whenever it was dark, he would come in to try to reassure me. "See," he'd say, turning the lights on, "they're not real animals." After a couple of rounds of trying to prove what was real and what wasn't, I'd be left to fend for myself.

Now that my father is upstairs in bed, I open up my mother's travel diary that I've taken from her suitcase. As always, she's recorded her travels efficiently, offering details in case she might someday have to report back to a friend or acquaintance. The travelogue reminded me of the letters she used to conscientiously send me at camp. "Saw a movie . . . ate dinner afterwards . . . played bridge with such and such . . . the weather was nice today."

I look quickly at the pages from early February when they had first arrived in New Zealand, and then skim ahead to Australia, closer to the weeks before she died. "Victoria Vista in downtown Melbourne is satisfactory and conveniently located," she's recorded. "Compare has good Italian food, bistro style." They'd made a week's trip to Bali before returning again to Australia, to visit the Great Barrier Reef. On February 26th, they stayed at the Village Hotel, "pleasant with a pool and outdoor sitting area. I seem to have gotten the popular 'Bali belly,'" she notes. "Joel ate dinner. I ate soup." On the 27th they attended a local wedding. "The people were extremely hospitable and offered us refreshments." On the 28th, their last day in Bali, they visited a volcano, and later did some shopping. "We bought a couple more boxes and carved ducks." It's hard to get a real picture from my mother's documentation. But then uncharacteristically she writes, "The night of the 28th was sleepless. We'd had a difficult landing due to a storm. I was never so terrified in my life!" My father had mentioned that, too, how frightened my mother had been on the flight from Bali back to Australia. He told Ted that when the plane dropped in an air pocket, my mother had dug her fingernails so deeply into his arm it had left marks. She told my father she was worried she'd never see her children or grandchildren again. I shiver at the premonition.

On March 1st, it was raining in Cairns and they did their laundry. "It's a day of relaxing," she reports. "A good dinner at George's Athenian Restaurant." On March 2nd it was still drizzling. They'd taken a gondola ride over the rainforest and went to a butterfly sanctuary. "Later a delightful cruise viewing the wildlife—Kauri trees, softshell snapping turtles, eels, various birds."

The last entry is for March 3rd. She must have written it the night before when she'd closed her diary, in anticipation of the next day. "The Great Barrier Reef," it's titled, and the rest is a blank page.

≈

We're going ahead with the funeral. My mother's body still won't be released from Australia for another few days, so we've decided to go ahead with the ceremony, and leave the burial for when the body returns. Roy and the kids are now with me in Andover. Eli and Eva nestle beside me on the blue and orange couch. I turn the pages of the photo album, showing them old pictures of my mother. She looks more beautiful than I'd remembered. Once when we were teenagers or in our twenties, Ted and I were talking about our childhood, and Ted wistfully said he had always thought, "Mommy was the most beautiful woman in the world." I was amazed at his image of my mother. To me, she always had her immensity, but it was usually more as an obstacle than a beautiful vision.

I put Eli to sleep in Ted's old bedroom, tucking him in with the brown, fake fur bedspread that my mother had once made to go with the brown and white zigzag striped wallpaper. "It's like Grandma Lois is still here," Eli says.

"Her love is still here," I try to explain.

"She's up in the sky," Eli tells me right back. "Her love is in the moon and the stars."

"Her love will always be here." I can't believe I'm saying and even believing these words as I kiss my son goodnight. My mother's spirit is turning into something more mystical than I would have expected from a practical person like my mother. It's as if I'm being tripped up about how exactly to remember her.

Once Eli, Eva, and Roy are all upstairs sleeping, I'm alone with my father in the living room, remembering my mother. "She was so good," my father says. I can see from the look in his eye that for him my mother has already become transformed in the few days since her death. An idealistic take on reality is not unusual for my father, a true rose-colored glasses man. "She never liked arguing," I hear my father's voice blending into illusion. "Whenever I was angry with her, she tried to stop me from being angry," he says. "She just couldn't stand fighting." I almost smile at the way he can twist the truth, but it's exasperating, even if she *has* died.

Can my father possibly have forgotten that celebration of my mother's sixtieth birthday? That cold weekend in May, when we took that wretched trip to Cape Cod. It was a few years after Danny had died, and we hadn't spent much time together—the four of us alone. It was hard to be together in those first years without Danny, hard to bear each other. But we had to do something to mark my mother's birthday. We took hikes, single file, across the cedar board planks through the dunes, half-heartedly commenting on the berries and shrubs along the way, noticing an occasional bird. My mother and I ventured off by ourselves onto the windy beach, and immediately she made use of the opportunity to launch into a tirade against me. I was way too picky. *That's* why I wasn't married. Why did I think I was so special? She made no attempt to hold back, sinking into self-pity in the way she only seemed to do with me, at my expense. It was an embarrassment that she didn't have grandchildren like all of her friends did, she told me. It was *my* fault that *she* was unhappy.

"You're mean!" I shrieked at her, into the cold beach air. And I meant it with every piece of myself. Just like I had all those nights as a child when I'd sobbed in my bed because she was such a miserable mother. Never seeing me for who I was. Preferring that I be invisible rather than get in the way of who she wanted me to be. And even that was impossible to get right. I was too shy, too skinny. My hair was too curly, even though she had curly hair, too. My hair was impossible because it was thick and unmanageable. Wasn't my best friend Susan's long red hair beautiful? she'd ask. I had to agree that Susan's hair *was* beautiful. Would she have preferred to have Susan as a daughter? Susan's mother would carefully braid her hair, something my mother would never do, and in the summer Susan's mother put her hair up with barrettes in a kind of bun that she called a "fan." I begged my mother to let me have long hair, too.

"She didn't mean it," my father would say when he'd come to console me after yet another one of our screaming arguments. He'd try to get me to stop sobbing, so I would fall asleep. "Just apologize to each other," he'd say. But what had I done wrong? I'd never apologize, and neither would my mother.

My mother had her ideas for me, for how my life might turn out alright. Some of her suggestions were that I could teach kindergarten, or work in a school for mentally retarded children. My mother saw these as things I could do before I got married. She liked it when I did volunteer work one summer at camp, in fact working at a home for mentally retarded children, at a place that was unbelievably depressing and was closed by the state a few years later. In high school when I did an internship at a rehabilitation center for the mentally handicapped, mostly to avoid going to class that last semester, my mother saw that as worthwhile, too. The more depressing the work, the better, it seemed. One summer during college when I couldn't find a waitressing job right away, a local nursing home offered me work cleaning toilets. My mother thought it was a big mistake to turn that down. "It's a paying job," she pushed. "Take it."

When I graduated from college I was unwise enough to tell her I wanted to work at something I loved. I wasn't sure of exactly what that was, but something that had to do with art. Like writing, or painting. "Grow up!" she said back. "This is the real world. What makes you think you get to love what you do?" For years I was stuck somewhere in the middle, trying out different graduate schools, a stint at a rare book auction house, and another job as an editorial assistant. I'd never make quite enough money, and never really explored my dreams either.

"You're selfish! And you'll never get married," she cursed me on that bleak Cape Cod beach. "You'll never find some one to measure up to your high standards." If my mother were here now, she probably wouldn't remember any of it. Or at least she'd claim not to remember. That was one of the great est frustrations in dealing with her. We could have the most treacherous argument, and it would be as if it never had hap pened. Once I was considered safe—in this case married and the mother of two laudable children—the problem no longer existed. This was how my mother accomplished her life in a world of obstacles. This was how she endured.

≈

Seated in the limousine, we drive out of the maze of colonial houses in our neighborhood and turn onto Main Street, on our way to the synagogue for the ceremony. The big tree on the corner is still standing, still with the remains of the gash where Danny crashed into it the same week he'd gotten his license twenty years ago. Ironically, the small church parking lot where my father had taught us to drive is just behind the tree. Ted and I wince almost simultaneously.

"I don't think Danny hated this place like we did," I say to Ted. Ted agrees with me. "Danny really liked everything," he says. "He loved life." It might not make sense to say that someone who committed suicide at age twenty-two loved life, but it was true. When Ted and I could be ponderous, Danny was naturally playful. Even though he'd chosen death, before that, he seemed to align with life.

After Danny's funeral we'd all gathered under the big oak on the sloping front lawn of the house in Andover, sharing our memories. It was October, but the ground wasn't cold yet, and the leaves were in full color. Danny's friends from college were there, some less surprised than others about his death, but everyone shocked by it. His girlfriend put aside the several months of estrangement before he died, and recalled their more lively times, when they'd shared an apartment together a couple of summers earlier. Once she, Danny, and I had all driven together to the beach, laughing and singing the whole way. I recounted the New Year's resolution Danny had made the year before he died. "This year I want to learn how to share," he'd said. There had been so much yearning in Danny, so much effort to try to get life right.

My father, Ted, and I leave the private room off to the side where they keep the immediate family members before being ushered into the sanctuary. We take our allotted seats, in the front row facing the ark. The three rabbis are already sitting up on the *bimah*. I take a brief look behind me, and see the extended rows all filled with people—there may even be a thousand—all there to honor my mother. For my mother, this ceremony makes sense, nothing at all like when Danny died, when we were all so raw and any kind of ritual was ludicrous.

One of the rabbis starts crying when he speaks about my mother's accomplishments. Although I never would have imagined it, I am moved to tears, too, hearing about all of her many contributions to Jewish education, about all of the people who will miss her.

I make my way to the podium and my stomach rises at the sea of uncountable people in front of me. "My mother was large," I begin. "She was unstoppable." I tell the story of when my mother once tried taking a yoga class. It was in the '60s and all her friends were trying it, but she deemed the classes too boring to continue. She'd also once attended a consciousness-raising group, but saw no use in that either, saying it was "nothing but a bunch of women complaining about their problems." To this, I hear some laughter of recognition.

"I'm thankful that my mother died in a beautiful place," I continue. "It was by the beach." I try to tell the audience how my mother and I have finally connected, how we had come to understand each other. But then I start to feel shaky and the words no longer make sense. I wonder why it should matter that this sanctuary full of people know how I feel about my mother.

"a child

in her cotton dress

the lawn, the copper beech—"

The words of Louise Glück's poem that are supposed to be a tribute to the uncanny bond between my mother and me have lost their meaning. I step back down to my seat between my father and Ted.

Ted tells some happy family stories that make me smile, and the audience laughs. There are memories about how my mother used to talk on the phone for hours on end, how with the extra-long phone cord she'd been able to speak and at the same time prepare an entire dinner. There's a story of family lore about Uncle Joe, who used to laugh so uproariously at his own jokes that he'd cry, and another about how my mother, Cecile, Joe, and Nate used to go to the beach in Far Rockaway when they were children. But then, without warning, Ted bursts into a description of my mother's love for him. "Our mother's love was pure love," I hear him say, "simple love." And he really seems to mean it. It's like his picture of my mother as the most beautiful woman in the world.

I'm completely disarmed. I want to announce that what Ted is saying is impossible. I know for a fact that everyone in our family has experienced the debilitating web of anxiety that came with my mother's love, a love that was anything but simple" or "pure." There was that constant inescapable fear of hers that pervaded our household, providing an unspoken rule that everyone had to act like our world was perfectly okay, even though it was really an oppressive place where we lived, in a prison, as Danny called it. To survive all of that nervousness of my mother, you had to work very hard to rise above it, to breathe and look around. How could Ted possibly adore my mother this way in front of all these people?

≈

It's been a full week, and my mother's body has finally arrived from Australia, officially delivered in what's referred to as the "container." Now we will bury her. Roy and I argue about whether it's right to bring Eli and Eva to the cemetery. I say they should witness what's happening, even if they don't understand it. Eli already has preconceived notions about death, and it's best not to be mysterious. He already knows from the TV show *Arthur* that people and pets get buried underground, I reason. And Eva is probably too young to be fazed one way or another. But Roy says I need to be free to respond spontaneously, and not worry about the kids. I don't persist because maybe he's right, and really I don't know whether it's that important for the kids to see my mother get buried. Roy drops Eli and Eva off at the local indoor playground that happens to be run by a childhood friend of mine, where they both can be cared for and even get to play, and then he returns to drive us to the cemetery.

The cars gather first at the synagogue parking lot. This time it's all solemnity, no ceremony. I get out of the car to hug Nate and his wife Gail, who have flown up again for the second time this week from Washington. Aunts and uncles, and even many of my cousins have made the trip for the burial. Car doors are opening and slamming. It's cold, "raw," as my mother would say, typical of March weather in New England, but no one's wearing a coat because they've been driving from Boston and New Hampshire and New York, and they're all getting right back into their cars again. My parents' friends are already all lined up in a procession, ready to go. My father and Ted and I return to our small Volkswagen and huddle together in the back seat, and Roy starts the car.

When we enter the cemetry, I have no recollection of having been here before, even though it's where we buried Danny fifteen years earlier. As we approach the grave, my father, brother, and I with our arms linked, I vaguely recognize the place that has now become our family plot. The network of roots surrounding Danny's coffin has been freshly cut away to make room for my mother's coffin, which has already been lowered into the ground next to Danny.

After fifteen years of his festering death, my mother lies side-by-side with my brother in the ground. My mother no longer has any choice in the matter. There they are next to each other in their identical pine boxes, each with a small Jewish star carved on top, Danny's slightly darkened with age.

The rabbi says some brief prayers. My father, Ted, and I look down from above. We begin to fill in the dirt, each symbolically throwing in a shovel full, before the professionals take over. And then it's over, and it's time to go. After my mother's long journey, we leave her there in her coffin, next to Danny, the dirt and small stones tumbling on top of them.

≈

I need to find a copy of the Death Certificate before we return to New York. The man from Club Med told me if I could show him the certificate, they'd refund the tickets for our trip to the Bahamas that we were supposed to take the week after my mother died. The documents are all supposed to be in the big cardboard box, now sitting on my parents' kitchen table, shipped from Australia along with my mother in the container. There are supposed to be multiple copies included, but I can't find them, at least not right away. I do see an envelope stamped "Contents of the Container," and open it to find a list of everything contained in the box. One item looks peculiar: "The remains of the Honorable Funeral Director of Cairns, Australia." I think this must be a bureaucratic error, but I show it to Ted to be sure, and also because it strikes me as a little humorous. When I see a look of worry wash over Ted's face, I realize it's the same feeling I have. The reality is that when Levine Chapels called yesterday to ask whether any of us wanted to drive to Brookline to see my mother's body, for some reason it hadn't seemed necessary, and we'd all said no.

Ted picks up the phone and calls Levine Chapels, a number he now knows by heart. They assure him that they'd checked, that it was definitely my mother who was in the container, and she was there by herself.

If I could only now rush back to my mother's coffin and see for myself. To be completely sure that she's really in her grave.

Two

"Put your *keppele* down on the pillow," my grandmother would say when she put me to sleep. She'd stroke my head gently. "What beautiful curls," she'd say. I nestled into the big puffy feather pillow in its fresh case. It was like sleeping on a cloud. A cloud far away from home where I was used to hard, foam rubber pillows and scratchy wool blankets. I'd dreamily fade off in the big bed in her royal apartment that was right across the street from the Grand Concourse. In the morning there was sweet-smelling Palmolive soap in the bathroom. My grandmother told me stories about my father getting poison ivy, and how she had to scrub him down in the bathtub with some other kind of harsh soap that smelled bad, and how they couldn't switch back to the sweet soap for a whole week. I loved listening to the way she took care of my father when he was a little boy.

When I was only seven my parents let me go by myself to visit my grandmother in the Bronx. My father buckled me into my seat in the airplane at Logan Airport. And my grandmother was waiting to meet me when I walked down the ramp and onto the runway at Idlewild. There she was, dressed in her gray tweed suit, with the carved jade brooch pinned on the lapel, smiling to see me, just like always. After we dropped my suitcase at her apartment, we went right out again to Addie Vallins' soda fountain for a malted milkshake, the kind you could only get in the Bronx.

My hand in my grandmother's, she took me all around Manhattan that week. Way out onto the arm of the Statue of Liberty, to the top of the Empire State Building and on the Circle Line so we could see the whole city from a ferry boat. At Radio City, after the Rockettes, my grandmother got a little worried that the movie *Gigi Goes to Paris* might not be suitable. But on the huge screen of the miraculous theatre, Gigi was magnificent. Afterwards we went to Schrafft's, where the perfectly round scoops of chocolate ice cream were served in silver bowls.

My mother wasn't soft like my grandmother. She was brusque and efficient. When we got sick, it seemed like she was a little scared she might catch what we had. Not that she was ever irresponsible. She'd dutifully take our temperatures, give us baby aspirin and make sure that we drank plenty of liquids. Sometimes she'd even smash up the pink aspirin in a bowl of applesauce to get us to swallow it. She'd shake the thermometer really hard with a certain twist of her wrist to get the mercury to go all the way to the bottom, so the reading would be accurate. And when the thermometer read 98.6 for a full twenty-four hours, she sent us back to school the next day.

It seemed like being a mother might have been a difficult job for her, not that she ever said that out loud. It was as if she had to keep moving so she wouldn't have to think too much about what she was doing. At home with us she was always busy with cleaning the house, keeping it well-supplied as economically as possible, cooking praiseworthy and nutritious meals, and making sure that we were three well-functioning children—that we were healthy, went to school, did our homework, played our musical instruments, and that our teachers and friends and friends' parents all liked us.

"Teddy already knows how to read!" she told her friend Ellie on the phone. "Marcia Zelliger told me he was sitting on her front step with his book about the rabbit. He turned the page at the right place every time, and he could recite exactly which words were under each picture." Not only did my mother say that Teddy was smart, but the neighbor confirmed it. She talked about me on the phone, too, even if it wasn't about how smart I was. "I'm looking into art classes for Anne in downtown Old Marblehead," I might hear her say. The teacher chose her and one other girl to make the mural on the classroom wall, and now I'm thinking that maybe she should take art lessons. Joel can take her on Saturdays." She made it sound like we were model children she was proud of. Sometimes she'd give out recipes for her pastries—frosted brownies and apricot bars, and once in a while even her special recipe for rugelach, which people said was the best they'd ever tasted. Her friends all admired how good she was at taking care of us and at keeping the house in great shape.

I believed in her competent image, too. I was especially impressed by the way she could get into long conversations on the phone with people she didn't even know. It could be someone new in town who didn't know that the fish was freshest on Thursdays, or how to get a parking sticker for the beach.

Or she'd have a long talk with the kosher butcher about prices and cuts of meat when she placed her order each week.

She could appear to be a mother anyone would want. She'd laugh and smile and her body looked inviting, like I'd want her to hug me. And sometimes when she did, she was warm, and it seemed like she meant it. It was that feeling that always kept me coming back for more, that made me think I could find true comfort in my mother. But then just as surely as the soft form of my mother had been there, it would disappear with no notice at all. It was as though there were a goal bigger than being our mother that took her attention away. Things like buffing the kitchen floor once the wax had dried, or making sure that she hadn't missed a coupon for something she needed at the store that week, could sometimes seem more important than anything. The very fact that I wanted more of her could somehow be turned around into a negative trait. My very first word, she reminded me more than once, was "more." "It makes sense," she said. "You can never get enough!" Not only did I seem to have a character flaw, in my mother's opinion, but worse than that, "more" was confirmed to be unobtainable.

Deep down, I thought, my mother wasn't completely happy with being a mother. It was as if she wanted more, too, or at least something different. Maybe, I hoped, she'd change and be happier. And maybe someday she'd tell me about what it was like when she was a little girl. I couldn't put my finger on it, but there was something about the way she avoided talking about her mother and father that made me feel like she was always holding something in reserve for later. I knew that growing up her whole extended family lived in a brownstone on East 89th Street, her aunts, uncles, and grandparents on one floor and she, her brothers, sister, and parents on the floor above. I knew what the place looked like and felt like because my great-grandmother lived there until she was ninety, and usually we'd stop by for a visit when we came to New York. It was dark and dusty and old, with heavy red drapes and a big, solid, dark wood table. That's where we always sat, my great-grandmother shrunken and tiny, always wearing a turban on her head, covering what I'd heard was very long gray hair, all wrapped up inside. And there was a tiny garden in the back, with lots of old vines and weeds, and no flowers that I can remember. My grandmother Anna and grandfather Abe were shadowy. I never even knew what they looked like until Cecile had the old photographs copied and distributed to the family members when I was about eighteen. There were a few stories about how Nate got lost on the beach and how Cecile found him, or how Joe threw the package of Mallomar cookies out the window when he discovered they were made with gelatin and weren't kosher. But it was hard to imagine what their lives were really like.

Repeatedly, I'd ask my mother about how her parents died. But there wasn't much information on that either. "Cancer," she'd say quickly for my grandmother, and "heart attack" for my grandfather. One word for each. It didn't possibly seem like that could be the whole story.

When I was pretty young, maybe six or seven, my mother would tell me, "I never want to be a burden to my children when I get old." I used to wonder why she'd say that. It was as though she was taking me into her confidence, but also I thought there might be a tinge of blame in her words, something to do with *our* being a burden to *her*. When I think about it now, working as a Hebrew school principal might have come more naturally to my mother than taking care of us. Trapped with us at home, she didn't have the advantage of fully showing her exterior self. At the Hebrew school, she grew in stature from teacher to principal to very important principal. In the end, she was respected when she retired, just as she wanted. Even when she died, she appeared to be in perfect health, seemingly without a cause, and no one ever did have to take care of her. That was probably lucky because it's hard to imagine what it would be like to have to take care of my mother.

The fact was that my mother was almost always healthy. I remember her having the flu two or three times, and the occasional very bad cold, but she always seemed to recover fast. There was one time, though, when she got in a bad car accident when we lived in Connecticut. She'd gone through a yellow light and another car crashed into her, and her head hit the windshield. She was certain that the light had still been yellow. The police had to bring her home in a police car. They escorted her right up to the front door, and waited until she got inside before they left. There were black stitches on her lip. You could see the threads. For the whole next week she had to drink all of her meals through a straw because her lip was so swollen. Not just beverages, but soups, too. Everything had to be in liquid form. We thought of all the possible flavors of Carnation instant milkshakes she could have, and argued about who would get to shake the can for her. But she didn't see the fun of it. She refused to laugh, maybe because her lip hurt too much.

Sometimes my mother would actually cry. And when that happened, it was upsetting. Her face would contort into an unattractive form, her features slowly shifting until they finally registered into full-blown sobs. The way she'd look when she cried never made you want to console her. Usually the reason was because no one helped her with the house cleaning. She'd be in the living room surrounded by the old Electrolux vacuum cleaner that she swore by, and the carpet sweeper, which was lighter to handle and you didn't have to plug it in. My mother had a system for which surfaces required vacuuming and which ones got the carpet sweeper. In truth, I helped a lot with the carpet sweeping. It was fun to roll it around, and to clean out the clumps of dust wound up with the threads and other odds and ends that got stuck in the bristles.

Once when my mother was in one of her cleaning frenzies, she sponged down everything in sight on Danny's desk, which he'd arranged so carefully. She even wiped the tips of the wooden matchsticks that Danny had decorated, each with a different letter written on it, and the cork tops of the bottles he had filled, each in a different shade of water tinted with food coloring. She used that same stinky sponge on everything—furniture and delicate items alike, sometimes leaving little green crumbs of sponge on the surfaces. Danny was upset that the tips of the matches now smelled like sour sponge and that some of the letters had been wiped off. I felt bad, too, knowing how Danny must have felt. When she wiped everything clean like that, it was like she was making you invisible.

Danny wouldn't stay angry long, though. That wasn't his nature. That's why it was hard to stay mad at him, even though he could be infuriatingly impulsive. Like the time when he painted a portrait of Woody Allen right on top of the canvas I'd made a couple of years before, a picture of a tree with twisted branches. It was part of the oil paint kit I'd received as a birthday present when I was ten. At first I was furious, but when I looked at the portrait, which he had hung over his desk, I had to laugh, particularly because the resemblance to Woody Allen was really good for a kid Danny's age.

When my mother did cry, it would usually take place just around the time when my father returned from work. That way she could solicit his sympathy. "I never get any help around here," she'd say in between sobs. "I just can't take it when they don't even clean their rooms. It's impossible to even open the doors with all of their clothes in balls on the floor." We didn't see how it could possibly be such a big deal, but then her whole body would start quivering and sobbing, and it seemed like we must have done something really horrible. Like we were to blame for making the world my mother had tried so hard to maintain completely fall apart. In the end we'd always promise to try harder to help with the cleaning.

The Sunday newspapers are spread over the dining room table. The kids are occupied, and Roy's making another pot of coffee. I've just cleared off all of the pancakes from the plates, and am thinking about pouring a fresh cup. We're trying to have a normal weekend morning. As I sit back down at the table, my father is spouting out the headlines of *The New York Times*, but I don't bother to respond and neither does Roy. I'm used to my father expressing his indignation about the world. I just grit my teeth and try not to say that he should just read to the newspaper himself so we can all have some peace.

My father has taken to visiting us regularly, every couple of weeks now that my mother has died. I know I should be more tolerant. He's hungry for company, I tell myself. During his first visits, he was mostly silent. Even though I know that his daily world must be completely turned around since my mother's life ended so abruptly, I'm still taken aback at just how completely deflated and pained he is. I'd never really thought of my parents as belonging together. My father seemed too wide-eyed and independent-minded for my mother, who was always slightly annoyed by his obliviousness to her version of reality, his shakiness as a breadwinner, and his hair-brained approach to his responsibilities of keeping the cars from breaking down and the lawnmower running. He'd often spend Saturday afternoons patching things together with glue, not ordinary household products like Krazy Glue or Ducco cement, but batches of epoxy he'd make in the basement. Even though my father was a chemist, my mother, ever efficient, seemed skeptical of his practical abilities.

When Danny died, my father could barely function and couldn't stop breaking into tears at the mention of his name, while my mother kept forging ahead, not talking about it. My father, Ted, and I would do our best to drop Danny's name into a conversation—a story about his life, how much we missed him, anything we could come up with to help keep him alive. But my mother would never bring up Danny. That was when I was almost certain that my father would break away from my mother, that he wouldn't be able to stand her unrelenting momentum any longer.

When I was young and kids' parents started getting divorced, I began to think for sure that my parents were not married to the right people. If they would each just marry someone else I thought our lives could be better, and we wouldn't have to keep hearing the same grating tone of my mother's voice when she always seemed unhappy with my father's behavior. But my parents never seemed to be quite like other parents. Habit or duty or something seemed to hold them together, even after what seemed like too big of a divide after Danny's death. Now when I witness my father's loss, I feel guilty about judging my parents' marriage the way I did. There must have been an ongoing dynamic that I just couldn't see, something that must have at least resembled love to make my father so broken without my mother.

Maybe it's a good sign that my father's again reeling out his commentary on the world news. What Ted and I refer to as his "selective hearing" seems to be back, too. For years now, it's been hard to know if he might really be turning deaf, or if he'd just prefer not to acknowledge something that didn't interest him. His obliviousness to the routine of our lives bothers me again just like it always has, like when he doesn't notice that everyone else takes their shoes off when they come into the apartment, except for him.

"Dad, please take off your shoes when you come inside, like everyone else," I tell him. "This is New York City, the streets are dirty."

"I'm more comfortable with them on," he says back, undaunted.

It's hard not to get annoyed. And now without my mother around to badger him, the nagging sound of my own voice seems louder than before.

Eli has had enough of his toy castle, and comes back to the table. "Papa Joel, tell me how Grandma Lois died. Did you see it happen?" He's right up close to my father, trying to look him in the eye. When he doesn't answer, I'm embarrassed of my harshness with my father. If he can hear, I'm thankful that he hasn't chosen to give Eli the details of what he saw.

Fantastically, my father appears not to notice my intolerance. In fact, what he seems to see is exactly the opposite. "You're always so supportive," he tells me when it's time for him to leave to go back home. "You're such a good daughter."

≈

I know the water will be chilly, but I have to make myself get into the pool again. I haven't been swimming once for the past month since my mother died. Finally, ID in hand, I walk over to the Columbia gym. I head straight for the locker room, change into my bathing suit, don't bother to take a shower first, and walk right up to the edge of the pool, which I know will be cold. In the first couple of laps, I find myself sputtering, but it's just the power of suggestion. Soon I'm swimming effortlessly.

To my complete surprise, I can feel my mother's presence with me in the turquoise walls of the pool. It startles me a little, because swimming has always been my private world. Even when my lane is crowded, and I need to gauge my speed against the other swimmers splashing past me in the lane, I'm there on my own. But now that I think about it, it was my mother who first took me to the water. Even though she wasn't much of a swimmer, she loved the ocean as much as I did. In those years when we lived in Marblehead, just as long as there was a little sun and the temperature hit seventy degrees, we'd head for the beach. I'd play in the waves or run further down the beach, while my mother kept an eye out. Maybe it makes sense that she's here with me now.

⁓

"Just wait two minutes while I get these apples chopped," I yell at Eli, who's grabbing his ball back from Eva.

"*My* ball, *my* ball." Eva starts crying.

The water for the eggs is boiling. I set the timer for eight minutes before picking up Eva to console her. I can't stand my voice, screaming at the kids as I try to prepare for our small Seder. My mother's tenseness rings in my head, as I attempt to recreate a small version of the Passover I grew up with, the holiday I always remembered with great anticipation. I must have helped my mother get ready for twenty or more Seders in my life, but it's been a long time since then and I'm no longer sure of the details. I found a children's Hagaddah coloring book around the corner at the bookstore, and there's a picture of what goes on the Seder plate. Roy doesn't like rituals, but he's agreed to go along with it, he says, as long as I don't take it too seriously. It's only the four of us, nothing demanding. I just want the kids to know a little bit about the story of Passover, I tell him.

Growing up I loved Passover. Every year we'd read from the same wine-stained Maxwell House Hagaddahs, everyone singing off key and no one caring because everyone was tone deaf. I can still taste the chalky yolks of the hardboiled eggs that would finally be passed around the table. We'd bathe them in the bowl of salt water along with the parsley, and slide them around on our plates and into our mouths. I didn't know how I'd possibly last another half hour until we got to eat the *charoset* and *maror* sandwiches made with broken pieces of matzoh. The whole extended family wouldn't be there like at Thanksgiving, but usually my aunt Cecile's family came, and sometimes Nate. Once, my great-grandmother even made the trip up from New York. Shy as I was in those days, when it was my turn to read from the Haggadah, I'd recite my lines in a strong voice. Sometimes my cousins and I took turns pretending to be Elijah, making objects move mysteriously or opening the door in spooky ways. One year Danny dressed up as Elijah's ghost.

My mother always constructed two delicious Passover meals, the first night turkey, the second night pot roast. She'd carefully shape the matzoh balls and drop them into the soup. It was a big operation to set the table. We had to bring out both of the extra leaves, and unroll the foam pads specially cut for the larger table shape before laying out the big tablecloth that was actually a striped Indian bedspread. I'd set the table with the special Passover plates and the tarnished silverware that we hauled out of the basement each year for the holiday. My mother was even more anxious than usual. I could feel her nervously watching to make sure I was using the right silverware, not mixing the meat with the milk. And there was always some worry about the matzoh balls being too heavy. One year she'd try adding club soda, and the next year it might be extra chicken fat. But she always managed to pull through right up to the sponge cake that she made with ground nuts.

One year, I discovered a reason why my mother might have been in a bad mood on Passover. My aunt Cecile told me that their mother died when she was seventeen and my mother was nineteen, and it happened the night before Passover began. Their rabbi invited the whole family—my mother, Cecile, Joe, and Nate, and of course their father, to his family Seder because their mother had just died. "I was so proud having the Seder with the rabbi that year," was what my mother told me when I asked her about it. But Cecile had said it was miserable, maybe the worst night of her life. And later Nate told me how scared he was that Passover night when he was only seven. Cecile also told me that when their mother was dying of breast cancer, she sat by her side during those final months, changing her messy bandages, while my mother was nowhere to be found. My mother did not like being around death.

Six years ago when I was visiting my parents on Passover, unbelievably my great-grandmother died the day before the holiday began. At 104, she was the oldest living member of our family, a true relic especially by our family's standards. She had outlived her own daughter by more than sixty years, but still she managed to die on the same day before Passover. "Isn't it peculiar that both your mother and grandmother died on the very same day of the calendar?" I pointed out to my mother. But she just gave me a blank look.

My great-grandmother had to be buried very fast in keeping with Jewish law. She was living in Crown Heights with Great-Aunt Gussie and her family, who had become Hasidic many years before. "It has to be before sundown," was what Gussie's husband Joseph had said. "We have to get her in the ground before Pesach begins."

My mother never made it to the funeral. She said it would be impossible to get back in time for our Seder. Cecile, Joe, and Nate all got to the burial in time, Cecile already being in New York, but Nate and Joe flew in from Washington. "They just threw her in the grave," was how Joe described it. That year, by chance, my mother had planned to have only family friends at the Seder, no relatives, so as it turned out everyone came, and Passover went on as planned.

With the help of the coloring book Haggadah, I tell Eli and Eva the story of the pyramids and Pharaoh and the slaves, and the parting of the Red Sea. And Roy chimes in with a verse of *Dayenu*.

After I've already kissed Eli goodnight, he calls me back into his room for one more last thing. "Why do we celebrate Passover for seven days?" he asks. I explain to him that the Jews spent seven days wandering in the desert before they could get out of Egypt. "So tell me, Mom," he says. "Moses was the good guy and Pharaoh was the bad guy, right?" By his standards he's exactly right, and I nod, happy to have accomplished something new this Passover.

~

My nerves are still frayed, and I keep on getting angry at the kids even though Passover has come and gone.

"*My* mommy, *my* mommy," they clamor and fight with each other every night as I make dinner. I try hard not to let my exasperation show.

"Mom, what makes you cry?" Eli asks me one morning on the way to school.

"When I'm very sad or hurt I sometimes cry," I tell him. "But not often—only some of the times when I'm sad or hurt."

"Do you ever get angry when you're sad?" he asks.

Eli's wisdom seems impossible for his four years. At forty-three, I'm only now starting to grasp that my mother's anger might have come from a deeper place, a place that might have more to do with sadness. I wish I'd known how to sympathize with my mother. Maybe then I'd know how to mourn for her. Sometimes I just want the kids to get out of the way, and Roy, too, so that I can go on with this act of grieving. But then in trying to remove the human obstacles from my path, I'm being like my mother, and I want to get rid of that, too. And how can I possibly grieve for my mother when I want to get rid of her?

After dropping Eli off at pre-school, it's only 8:30 a.m. and I see that Eva has fallen asleep in her stroller. With the whole morning still ahead of me, I wheel the stroller into Starbucks to buy an overpriced cup of mediocre coffee. I set myself up at a table and unload my backpack that's always filled with book proposals waiting to be read. The first one, as luck would have it, turns out to be a synopsis for a healthy Kosher cookbook. Coincidentally there's some kind of Middle Eastern music playing in the background, and I find myself weeping uncontrollably as my mother's presence suddenly and completely overwhelms me. All I need is time to remember her and be sad, I reason, so I won't be angry.

Roy wants to be supportive. I tell him we really have to take a trip to the Caribbean, the one we didn't get to take when my mother died, but he says he can't spare the time from work. It infuriates me that he's not being understanding. "How about we go to Cape Cod for a week this summer?" Roy suggests. He doesn't get it. The summer is still months away, and I need something immediate—the calm of clear lapping waves and fine white sand.

Then he says he'll take the kids to New Jersey this week-end to visit his parents, so I can have a day to myself, and he has it exactly right. When Saturday arrives, I pack the bag of snacks and toys for their car ride, and they leave.

I start out by opening the mail that's been mounting up on the chest of drawers in my bedroom. Right there in the enve-lope on the top of the pile is the rebate check from Club Med. I can't believe our good fortune. Now we really *can* turn around and use the check for a new vacation. I dial 1-800-Club Med, and book us for five days in the Bahamas later this month. I can easily envision the gentle Caribbean water.

But the Club Med reservation isn't really going to work out. I already know that. Roy's already said he can't take the time off from work now. And besides, when I check the flight possibilities, everything that's available is indirect, and changing planes with the kids would only be an ordeal, not relaxing at all. Still, I put the receiver back in its cradle and let the reservation sit for a few hours, enough time to really cry and feel sorry for myself. My mother is like a beach I can't get to. Now more than ever, she is nowhere to be found.

Three

"No shooting, no shooting!" Eli cries out. But his chest is already sopping wet where the older boy holding the huge water gun has doused him. Only moments before, Eli was shrieking with delight, running in circles around the jungle gym while two bigger kids wielding water guns and pistols chased him. I watch helplessly as his face shifts from excitement to tears of hurt and confusion. "I don't like that boy," Eli shouts. "I didn't want him to shoot." His disappointment is unbearable.

Even though it's May, there's a chill in the air. I take Eli upstairs to change into dry clothes and leave Roy in Riverside Park pushing Eva on the baby swings. The phone's ringing when we enter the apartment, and I think about just leaving it. But I pick up just in time to hear Ted's voice, just before the answering machine clicks in. Cradling the phone under my chin, removing Eli's wet shirt at the same time, I tell Ted I'll call him back later. But he keeps on talking and he won't stop.

"He's already six," Ted's saying about his son David. "It's time he knows how Danny died. It's a mistake not to have told him sooner." I'm confused about why he's talking about Danny right now, but then he abruptly switches to my mother. "They should know that she died in the water," he pronounces. "Secrets are not a good idea." He's planning to tell David and Karl, too, this afternoon.

"Can we talk about this later?" But there is no later. I try to get a word in edgewise, and to stifle my anger until after I hang up.

"I'm telling them this afternoon," he repeats. "About Danny, and about Mom. It's not a good idea to let any more time pass."

He has called to notify me, not to ask me. I'm furious. "I have to go," I say, and hang up the phone.

Eli's already busy playing in his room. I take a fresh towel from the bathroom and wrap him up and hug him, and try to forget about Ted and his righteousness.

"Why did those boys shoot?" Eli's asking again. It was just last week when Eli and I passed a man with a real gun. We were on the way to a birthday party and we were late, so we were walking fast when we saw a man pointing a pistol into the face of another man who was chained to a fence. I jumped. And then I saw there was a third man holding a camera.

"They're making a movie," I quickly explained to Eli. Eli's mouth was wide open.

"Was that a real gun?" he asked.

"They're just making a movie," I repeated. "They're pretending."

"Do people have real guns?" Eli asked.

"Some do."

"What do they do with them?"

I paused, trying to figure out how to answer. But Eli was already figuring it out. "They only shoot bad people, right?"

I nodded, relieved. Eli's view of the world was still intact.

It's such a delicate balance getting death in the right place. I don't want it always hovering beneath the surface of my children's lives like it was in my childhood. I want them to know about death, but not be consumed by it. Honesty is essential, that's always been my position. But not *over*-honesty. Not like what Ted's advocating.

I'm not ready to tell my kids that my mother died in the water. Eli's finally just begun swimming lessons, and Eva, who's still too young to swim, loves to splash around at the water's edge. Besides, we don't even know for sure how my mother actually died.

But it's the part about Ted talking to his kids about Danny that really has me enraged. There's no way I'd ever hold Danny's death as a secret. Ted knows that. I couldn't possibly allow the shadow of suicide to loom behind the scenes of my children's lives, like it did in our growing up. In that way, I know for certain I'm nothing like my mother.

Even before Eli was born, I'd thought about how I'd someday deliver the story of Danny's death to my children. I knew it would be a pivotal moment in our lives. Plunging ahead right now doesn't have to do with being honest. I'm sure this isn't the right time for it. And what if Eli now gets the news from his cousin? David's not much of a talker, so it's unlikely. But Ted's lack of sensitivity is infuriating. At four, Eli is definitely too young to learn about drowning, let alone suicide.

Ted can be like this sometimes. He can be unbelievably inconsiderate and think it's logical. He can make a unilateral decision that suits him and self-righteously storm ahead like it's good for the whole world. Like the time when he got angry at me for saying I wanted my own car back, the one I'd *lent* to him. I'd just moved back to New York, and could never find a parking space on the street for the little white Honda I'd bought (true enough, with my father's help on the down payment) during my days in Washington. So I told Ted he could use the car until I figured out what to do next. About a year later, when I managed to locate a parking garage I could afford way downtown, I told him I was ready to have the car back. And he actually said no, I couldn't have it. He couldn't possibly give it back to me now, not just when he was planning to *sell* it! Janet was pregnant and it hurt her back too much to have to lean over the seat when she was getting in, so they were planning to trade it in for a four-door car, he explained as though this was rational.

Growing up, Teddy and I were companions. We were only two years apart, and Danny wasn't born until Teddy was almost four. The two of us would spend hours in the basement, underground with the rusting pipes overhead and exposed stone walls surrounding us, while my mother took care of Danny upstairs. Sometimes my mother would bring down batches of homemade play dough that she'd make out of flour, water, and food coloring. It didn't have the same nice smell as the real stuff that came in a can, and it wasn't as spongy. But if you let it dry out and kept sprinkling water on it, you could shape it more delicately than you could do with real Play-Doh. I was the bossy older sister, so I got Teddy to run upstairs to get more cups of water, and I'd be in charge of building the villages we made in different shades of red and green dough.

In our underground world, we'd spend all afternoon practicing "Hush Little Baby, Don't Say a Word," preparing for the appearance we planned to make someday on TV on *Community Auditions*. I was the mother and I'd wrap Teddy in a plaid wool blanket and rock him on my lap while we sang. Once we got our own record player, our performances became more elaborate. We'd stage scenes from *Babes in Toyland*. Teddy would keep returning the needle to the same groove of the record until we got the song just right. I'd sing in my sweetest voice, "My sheep are gone for good, their cloaks our livelihood . . ." trying to get it just right, never sure of the exact words. Teddy would wander around, acting like my lost sheep, and I'd be Bo Peep looking for him in the corners of the basement.

When it wasn't too rainy or too bitterly cold, we'd play outside with the neighbors. In the winter, I'd break the icicles off of the low-hanging eaves of the roof and give them to Teddy, who would suck on them. There were a couple of winters when some elderly neighbors made their backyard into a skating rink for their grandchildren, and sometimes when it looked like no one was home we'd go over there and slide around in our rubber boots. In the spring we'd pick the red berries that we thought might be poisonous, and together we'd mix them with mud, saying it was chocolate, and try to feed them to the boy who lived at the far end of the street, even though we knew it was wrong. And when it got a little warmer we'd play hopscotch or kickball. When there was an argument about whether one of us had made it to the base before the ball, Teddy and I would usually stand up for each other.

United as the two of us could be, though, we were also different, and not always on the same side. He always knew how to follow rules and how to get along with my mother. My mother liked that Teddy and I were friends (maybe partly because it had the look and feel of a well-functioning family), but she also liked having Teddy for herself. She seemed to understand him more than she understood me. He was more predictable to her and safer, which was essential to my mother. I loved to walk on the edge of the curb, and there was an especially high one that went way up above the street near the doctor's office in Salem, where the streets were busier. "Get down now!" my mother would yell. But it was too much fun keeping my balance on the narrow stone curb high above the ground to come down. Teddy once told me he was amazed that I would just keep on doing what my mother said not to do. And I couldn't understand why he thought that was such a big deal.

Teddy may have been cooperative with my mother, but he could also make trouble. Once he tried to scare my father by creeping around the house in the middle of the night. The stairs started creaking and I heard my parents' door open. When I peered out from the bedroom that I still shared with Teddy, I saw my father treading around in the dark in his underwear, checking to see where the noise was coming from. He was walking very carefully in case it was a burglar or a murderer. He had a flashlight in one hand, and in the other hand he was holding the blown-glass bottle from the top of my parents' bureau. Just as he was about to start going down the stairs, Teddy jumped out and my father screamed louder than I'd ever heard and raised the glass bottle over his head. When he saw it was Teddy, he started yelling even louder and I was afraid my father might hit him instead of the burglar, but he caught himself at just the last minute. Teddy didn't like being yelled at, but he was pleased because he had won in tricking my father. I never would have thought to do anything like that, no matter how angry I was.

Teddy was very good in school. He was always in the smart class, and the teachers always thought he was one of the best students. I thought he might have taken a special test that told my mother he was smarter than Danny and me, because she always acted like she just expected Teddy to do better in school. My mother had been an excellent student, too. Once, she told us, her French teacher accused her of plagiarism because her essay was so far superior to anyone else's. Of course, the teacher was completely wrong because cheating was something my mother would never do. Another time, when she was in elementary school she got to go to Gracie Mansion because she won an award for her paper on why she was proud to be an American.

It was a little after Danny was born when Teddy started getting sick with a kidney disease and he had to go to the hospital. Sometimes he'd be at Children's Hospital in Boston for two weeks or even a month at a time. They'd attach wires to his brain and to his heart in tests called EEGs and EKGs. Once, my mother told us, they thought he might die, because he might have something called "water on the brain." That was when my mother obviously had to devote herself completely to Teddy.

Danny and I would stay home with a babysitter while my mother went to visit Teddy in the hospital. In the cold afternoons, I'd have to play outside without Teddy. I'd play tackle football in the backyard with a boy named Laurie, who was a year older and lived a few houses up the street. He was a lot bigger than I was, and he'd jump on me and drag me across the cold muddy ground whenever I tried to run to the goal, the forsythia bushes at the end of the yard. Sometimes my grandmother would visit from New York, and she'd be there to wipe off the mud and grass stains when I'd come inside to get warm. But most of the time, it was the babysitter who was there, an old woman with fluffy white hair and wrinkly skin named Mrs. Varrell, who would always be just sitting there, on the couch in the living room, attending to Danny in his pale yellow painted bassinet.

When I finished playing, I'd take over watching Danny. If he was asleep, I'd just look at him. I loved the way he'd hold onto his ear when he was sleeping. When he woke up, I'd very carefully hold him, or try to make him laugh. I tried to put my mother and Teddy out of my mind. I was the one at home taking care of my little baby brother.

When Danny was old enough to really form an alliance with me, sometimes we would observe Teddy, who would always fall asleep in the back seat of the station wagon when we'd go on long trips. He slept very deeply, and we'd touch his scalp and move it around with our fingers, feeling the bristles of his short whiffle haircut, testing how much pressure it took before he'd respond. Maybe if we prodded him in the right way, we'd be able to figure out what made him different from Danny and me.

Sometimes I'd test Teddy to see how long it would take to get him angry. I'd put my toe just inside the entrance to his bedroom to try to get him to respond. He could get incredibly mad, screaming and stomping around his room. He wasn't always completely good. Once when he was in third grade, he actually ran away from home. My mother went driving around in the car to look for him. She found him walking around the parking lot of the shopping center that was almost a mile away. But my mother didn't get on edge with Teddy the way she did with me and Danny. She just seemed to love him more, even before he got sick.

I know I'll call Ted back eventually, or he'll call me. No one really wants to walk away. Our reflex is still to be close, even if things are tense. For a while I thought it was when he got married to Janet that we began to go separate ways. That was when he clearly started creating a world separate from mine, maybe a place he could count on. It was around then that I realized we weren't talking much about the details of our lives anymore. We stopped sharing our friends like we used to. And we didn't agree as much as we used to about our views of the family. When I really try to trace it, though, the point when Ted and I started going separate ways was when Danny died.

With Danny's death, I felt like I'd lost my child. "Losing a child like that must be the worst thing that could ever happen to a mother," friends would say, when I'd tell them about Danny's suicide. "How can your mother stand it?" I'd nod back with a lump in my throat because to me, really I was the one who had lost Danny. And when my mother showed only blank emotion, it reinforced my role. In my pain, I not only yearned for Danny, but I hated my mother for her lack of sensitivity about the death of her own son. It remained my job to take care of him.

I could still hear Danny pleading with my mother to understand him, making her listen to the words of the Karla Bonoff song: "There's a rose in the garden. / It will bloom, if you're sure. / That you pay close attention / but leave it room." "I'm the rose," he'd tell her, playing the album over and over. It was the kind of thing my mother would laugh off as being ridiculous.

After he died, more than ever, it was my mission to be there for Danny, no matter how much my mother refused to hear.

Ted's response to Danny's death was different. He didn't seem to blame my mother for not understanding Danny the way I did. Besides that, the loss must have been distinct because as brothers he and Danny separately shared certain things—the same bedroom, the same overnight camp in New Hampshire where they climbed the same mountains, and the same college, although that was a place where Ted achieved, and Danny ultimately failed. As brothers they were also competitors, and Ted had the ability to succeed in places where Danny couldn't—in school, in getting my mother's attention, and ultimately in being alive. I worried about how hard it must have been for Ted to live with that. After Danny's death, Ted seemed to try hard to remind himself of how much the two of them had in common. He told me he "admired my pain," after Danny died.

With my mother's death, it seems we experience it differently, too. Just like in life, clearly Ted feels my mother's love, while I still struggle to find the ways to feel her presence. Ted remains allied with my mother, and I'm left grappling with whether she loved me enough. As much as Teddy and I shared growing up in our childhood home, we could also be two siblings on different sides. In the face of death, our differences are stronger.

Four

Two summers before Danny died, the three of us decided to take a trip together to Nova Scotia. I was living in a tiny studio apartment in Greenwich Village at the time. The place was so small you could see everything you owned in the world from any one spot, whether you were in bed or sitting at the table in the kitchen alcove. But I loved it because it actually had a working fireplace and it was in a great location right over Bradley's Bar. Most of all I was happy to finally have a place all to myself without any roommates. And I could manage the rent on my small salary at the rare books auction house where I worked. I didn't mind that the music from Bradley's sometimes shook the room. Or think it was strange when occasionally a policeman would dash by on the rooftop adjacent to my open window, looking for a criminal on the run. I was now on my own in the world, well out of my parents' home, college dorms, graduate programs, and now even without a roommate. The slightly precarious setting wasn't all that disturbing because for all the comforts of home that I'd known so far, the real security underneath had always been a little shaky.

I spent most of the time at my job describing engravings of bugs and botanicals in as many different ways as I could, to make the auction catalogues seem interesting. And I was looking forward to taking a couple of weeks off. Ted was on break from medical school in Cincinnati. And Danny, who was living in Providence, was also on summer vacation, although he thought he might not go back to Brown full time in the fall because it was getting tougher for him to concentrate on his courses. He thought maybe if he switched his major to Environmental Studies, he'd be more interested, but he wasn't sure. Two years before, when Ted had stayed on for an extra year at college to take science classes so he could apply to medical school, he'd overlapped with Danny in Providence. That was a while ago, but Ted said that Danny seemed fine, a lot happier at Brown than he was in high school in Andover. He lived in a house with his girlfriend and five other friends, too. Sometimes I'd see them when they'd come to New York together to go to Grateful Dead concerts.

Our plan was to drive the old blue Datsun that my parents had recently handed down to Ted, now that it had almost 200,000 miles on it. We'd drive the five hours up to Bar Harbor and then take the ferry the rest of the way to Nova Scotia. We met in Andover at my parents' house, and loaded all of our stuff into the car. One of my mother's friends commented on how nice it was that her three kids were going off on vacation together. I doubted it would be as pleasant as my mother's friend had in mind, but I admit to feeling forti-fied by the idea of the three of us together on this trip. That summer we all looked alike. We each had lots of curly hair, and Ted and Danny looked particularly unruly with scraggly beards. We knew we'd stand out in the territory we'd be covering, where we pictured most of the people to be fair-haired and mild-mannered. There was something about the trip that made me feel like the three of us together had a distinct place in the world. I wasn't exactly sure about Danny, but I was pretty certain that Ted agreed with me. There was even something vaguely symbolic about it, the three of us driving away and leaving our parents behind in the driveway.

When we left we were on edge, even though we didn't realize the extent of it. I'd already begun receiving some late night calls from Danny, asking me pointed questions about my childhood eating habits—which color foods I ate most and which textures were the most satisfying—or about the state of the environment. And once or twice he was really freaked out when he was crashing from a particularly bad drug trip. But by the time I'd call back to check up on him a couple of days later, he'd already moved on, so I didn't let it worry me too much.

Before we left, the only thing I could find for breakfast in my parents' kitchen was a frozen Lender's bagel, which I tried to pry open with a knife so I could get it to fit in the toaster. In the process, I sliced my thumb badly and had to double bandage it. It kept on bleeding right through the adhesive, and was still throbbing when we got into the car.

Once we were on the road, Ted and I discovered that Danny was now living according to a new code. He no longer showered, rarely changed his clothes, ate only bland food, and he told us that he never drank alcohol. He talked nonstop as we drove the five hours to Maine, lecturing us about his philosophy of food consumption and cleanliness. Whenever we'd get to a tollbooth, Danny would lean out the window to say thank you to the man who was taking our ticket, even though Ted was driving and he'd already done a perfectly good job of thanking the tollbooth attendant.

It was a lot different from the last family car ride we'd taken from Andover to New York several Thanksgivings ago, when Danny was still really funny, when my mother was sitting in the front seat, knitting as usual, and my father was of course driving. Danny had recently acquired a new tape recorder, and he would amuse us by periodically leaning over into the front seat to interview my mother about the progress of her sweater, part of a kind of running documentary he was making of the trip. "What's that you're knitting, Lois?" Danny would ask. She'd respond because she had no choice but to try to play along. "It's a baby sweater for my friend Ina's new grandson," she'd say without humor. Danny would press on. "Is that the elbow you're up to now, Lois?" When we got to a tollbooth, he'd bend over the window, microphone in hand, to get a few words from the tollbooth operator, who predictably would never respond. "Not a very friendly toll man," Danny would comment into the microphone in a droll voice. And we'd all laugh.

There was something about Danny's funniness and his ability to get us all laughing that held us together as a family. He pushed things a little, which got us out of what could otherwise be a depressing shell. Except for my mother. She didn't always want to play along with Danny's antics. Sometimes she'd cooperate and laugh nervously at his jokes. And other times when she couldn't take it, she'd shout at him to just shut up.

Danny was a great mimic, and sometimes he'd make up his own characters to impersonate. One was an impossibly short man named Herman Wasserman, who could perform the feat of reciting the alphabet at a phenomenal speed in a high squeaky voice. He also had a routine as a sportscaster at a fake tennis match played between an Israeli and an Australian, and he'd get everything from the accents to the weather conditions down perfectly. My mother, maybe rattled by the insulting description of the Israeli, would start screaming at Danny to stop bothering her, which Danny would then gleefully record with his new tape recorder. Danny had a full audience that Thanksgiving dinner at Aunt Cecile's, when he played the recording in front of the whole family. Everyone laughed hysterically, except for my mother who was mortified at the sound of her voice yelling at Danny at full volume.

On the drive to Maine, Danny was intent on getting us to fight. And not only with him. He seemed especially satisfied when he'd succeed at sparking an argument between Ted and me. It was an hour or so into the trip, Ted and I were in the front seat, and I was getting tired of craning my neck to respond to Danny, who was sitting behind us, spewing out his lectures. So I climbed into the back to sit next to him. But then I couldn't stand that either, and soon I was yelling at him and pushing him to move into the front seat with Ted, so that I could get some peace. We stopped at a diner for a second breakfast and a change of scenery, and after eating the spongy stacks of pancakes covered with too-sweet syrup, we only felt worse. By the time we reached Bar Harbor, I didn't see how we could possibly continue with our so-called vacation. Ted and I agreed that if Danny didn't stop battering us with his rules of life, we'd have to turn around. We decided to give it until morning.

Ted and I pitched the tent, my cut thumb really painful now as I hammered in the stakes, while Danny sat by the side, listening to music through his headphones and picking up his copy of *The Electric Cool-Aid Acid Test* from time to time. He was obsessed with the '60s, always regretting that he had missed that world by only a few years. Once we'd managed to put up the tent, we drove into town and went our separate ways to find food for dinner. Ted and I happily stopped at a hamburger place, while Danny went in search of fulfilling his vegetarian diet. There weren't many vegetables to be found in Bar Harbor, he told us. So he kept to pale foods—potatoes, oatmeal, bread.

The next morning we made it onto the ferry, and with the huge swells in the water, we realized that we'd hit the aftermath of a storm. Ted and I looked at each other's nauseated faces for the next few hours as the boat rolled over the ocean. We kept on changing our minds about whether to stay outside on the deck in the cold or go into the cabin, which was filled with other passengers with green-hued complexions and a growing stench that made it even worse. Mostly, we stayed outside, clutching ourselves in the chilling wind. Danny alone was unaffected by the seasickness, and he was happy to remind us why. "It's because your minds are not at peace," he'd say. "That's why you feel sick, you know." Then he'd go back to reading his book.

In Nova Scotia we rented a canoe in a national park and paddled along a river, like we were supposed to do on a vacation. The water was still and brackish and not particularly beautiful. We found ourselves drifting away from the other canoes, and before we knew it we were headed straight for a family of beavers. There they were right in front of us, slapping their tails against the muddy banks. We panicked, thinking they were about to come after us. And for once, the three of us banded together, even if it was in fear, and quickly paddled back up the river to safety. Back in the car, we agreed that the landscape was less beautiful than we'd expected. The tourist sites reminded us of trips we'd taken with our parents growing up. We made fun of my mother and father, who always stopped to read every sign in front of a fort or a bridge, or what might have once been the site of a battlefield. They'd dragged us to museums and even factories in the most unlikely places. There had been the fiberglass boat-making place somewhere near Cape Cod. And the Beechnut Lifesaver and Gum factory in Upstate New York.

And there had been the visit to Corning Glass during the vacation to the Finger Lakes. As we viewed the huge vats of hot, molten substance, we suddenly realized that Danny, who was only four or five at the time, was nowhere in sight. My mother went into a frenzy, and we all started tearing around the gigantic factory, each taking a different route in hope of finding Danny. My mother imagined the worst and even made my father get someone to page Danny on the loud speaker. After about an hour, we gave up and in desperation headed back to the car. My mother said we'd probably have to contact the police. In the immense parking lot, we finally located our car. And there was Danny, sitting on the pavement next to it. None of us could figure out how he possibly had been able to find it. "I knew you'd never leave without the car," he'd explained.

Something about Danny was always a little bit at stake, something that kept the family on its toes. Even though he was my little brother, he was my champion, always creatively breaking the family mold that could be so oppressive. My role was to take care of him and to egg him on, so he would always be able to play his clever tricks.

Once we reached Cape Breton, we knew why we'd driven all of this way. It was enchantingly beautiful, green and craggy. We learned that the immigrants who'd once settled here from Scotland and Brittany were drawn to the place because of its familiar terrain. And they remained stuck in time to this day, the French and the Scottish still in their separate communities, keeping many of their seventeenth-century customs, and still speaking incomprehensible versions of their original languages, still allured by their homes of centuries ago through the beauty of Cape Breton.

At last we were quiet. About to begin our hike along the pink granite rocks looking out onto the ocean, Danny took out a stick of deodorant he'd been carrying with him in his jacket pocket, and surprised us by unfolding the magic mushrooms that he'd carefully hidden, wedged into the bottom of the stick of Old Spice. I was relieved that Ted and I hadn't known about the mushrooms when customs had checked our bags at the border. We ate them, Danny's gift to us. The flavor was particularly foul mixed with the deodorant taste. As we hiked along the pink and black speckled rocks, the hard surface beneath our sneakers grew softer with our steps. Nature shed all traces of fear as we descended down to the water's edge, where we found lovely little coves and secret beaches. Ted and I became lost in our world of remembering the perfection of childhood at the beach, until we suddenly noticed that Danny was missing. Inexplicably, we were filled with acute alarm. We furiously called out for him, hoping that our voices would echo into the surrounding woods.

In time Danny mysteriously appeared, emerging from a wooded hollow and entering our cove. He had just decided to take a walk by himself, he told us. Of course he'd come back.

When we rushed to him and told him how worried we'd been that we'd lost him, he remained calm and a little intrigued. "But you don't *really* need me," he said. Even then it was an unnerving comment, and we poured out our disagreement. We absolutely meant what we said, Ted and I told him. We needed the three of us to have the right balance. It was essential. "You should read *The Waves* by Virginia Woolf," I told Danny. We were all part of one whole, and without one of us the whole wouldn't work. Ted and I worried that we had to explain this. Danny told us we were wrong, that the quietude Ted and I remembered at the beach of our childhood was something he'd never felt. This couldn't possibly be true, Ted and I insisted. We had to remain together. Without one of us, our equilibrium would be lost. But there was more than a shred of uneasiness that the connection we were demanding from Danny just wasn't there.

On the way home, we took the long route, driving the whole way rather than taking the ferry, and we weren't fighting anymore. I kept on thinking about how it must have been for Danny to be a child in our family. I now realized that he'd been only four when we left Marblehead. Maybe he really hadn't felt the waves and the sand and the freedom of playing at the beach during the long summer days like Ted and I had. Danny was only a baby, just learning to talk when he sat on the beach blanket next to my mother and her friends. He'd call my mother "Lotus" instead of "Lois" or "Mommy," and my mother and her friends would laugh at how cute and funny he was.

Everyone loved him. But maybe he never really got that part. While I was battling my mother's on-again, off-again presence, maybe Danny never really sensed her traces of love.

Maybe it was only my mother's imposed sense of order that he felt, a force that needed to be broken. Maybe the reason he was out there making sparks was because he needed some kind of proof of love he could never find.

When we crossed the border this time, the customs official pulled our car over to search us. The mushrooms were gone by now, and we had nothing to hide. We were incensed at being singled out by the authorities. They took us aside while they searched our trunk and our bags. Why didn't they pick on the short-haired man in the suit with his attaché case sitting in the car behind us? we joked. Eventually we made it through the investigation, but then we couldn't get the old Datsun to start, and had to leave the car with the customs officials to be towed to the nearest gas station. We spent the next few hours in that border town, eating ice cream in an old-fashioned ice cream parlor from the 1950s, until our broken-down car was fixed. For the time being, the three of us were together again.

≈

On my first birthday after my mother's death I'm determined not to sink too low. I love that my birthday marks the very beginning of summer. And the sky on this June day is perfectly clear, the air warm. I haven't been able to reschedule a publishing meeting that I have to attend. But I've made an appointment for a pedicure, so after the meeting I can walk around with toenails newly polished for the season. I wander around the streets aimlessly, in and out of stores, wasting time until Roy and I meet for dinner.

As we sit across from each other at our table in a restaurant in an elegant East Side townhouse, Roy takes my hand as he sees the tears start to well up in my eyes. "I miss my mother," I say. And he nods back with understanding. "You may be better off missing her," he says, his clear blue eyes looking straight into mine. I'm surprised at the forthrightness of his consolation. But I think I know what he means.

Roy comes from another planet from me when it comes to family hysteria. Maybe it's part of what keeps us steady—that he doesn't get drawn into the intense emotion or the frustration of seeking reasons that may not exist. It's taken some adjustment for him to grasp just how easily a birthday dinner with me can turn into a pool of sobbing. A few months after we met, when we celebrated my birthday together for the first time, he had to pay the bill quickly and lead me out of the restaurant in a stream of tears. Later he told me he was not only baffled, but really disturbed.

Each June for my birthday, my grandmother used to arrive with armfuls of dresses that she'd bought for me at Alexander's and a big white box of butter cookies shaped like little daisies with raspberry jam in the center. Every year she'd make a strawberry shortcake with lots of whipped cream between the two yellow layers and cover it with ripe red strawberries. It was special for my birthday, she told me, because strawberries were in season now that summer had begun.

Even though I believed my grandmother, that my birthday was special, the happiness of the day itself was always invisibly unsettled. My mother would always act like it was my birthday and she'd do everything that could be expected to celebrate. There would be a party with all of my friends, who would come and sit around the dining room table and sing "Happy Birthday." We'd eat the chocolate cake with white frosting and colored jimmies that my mother made each year, and the chocolate and vanilla Hoodsie ice cream cups that came with little wooden spoons wrapped in white paper that everyone had at their birthday parties. But even though my mother seemed to be smiling as she put the little paper party baskets on each plate, I could tell that she was more tense than usual on my birthday. And without fail, I'd end up in tears by the end of the day, even though we'd played pin the tail on the donkey on the side of the garage and gotten wet running under the sprinkler, and everyone had been excited when I'd opened the presents on the picnic table in the backyard. There was always something to set off a sense of disappointment, of expectations not met. It could be that a friend had slighted me in some small way, or that I didn't like a present I was supposed to enjoy. Whatever it was, the proportions would always grow way too big, and it was almost impossible for my birthday to turn out right. And the worst part was that I didn't want it to be sad.

Eventually it emerged that my grandfather had died the same week I was born. And I surmised that this must be why my mother was so on edge at the time of my birthday. "That's why I couldn't sit *shivah*, with the rest of the family," my mother at last revealed to me. "I had to be with you because you were a new baby." She said this with a certain weariness. "Tell me again how he died," I'd ask one more time. Predictably she'd again say, "heart attack." And like always, I could tell she really didn't want to talk about it. Still there was something about the plainness of her answer that made it seem like something was missing. "Was he the only one in the family to die of that?" I'd ask. So far, the other causes of death in the family that I knew of were cancer for my grandmother, complications from diabetes for my father's father, and something to do with a broken hip for my great-grandfather, who died when I was in second grade. No, she'd say, there were not any other heart attacks that she knew of.

Even after I discovered the truth about my grandfather, that in reality he'd committed suicide that third week in June when I was born, even after my mother knew that we all knew it, she kept up the heart attack story. When Ted had a relapse of his childhood kidney disease the summer when he was on break from medical school, he happened to be visiting my parents when he needed to check into the hospital. "Maternal grandfather?" the admissions nurse had asked as she filled in the family history on Ted's chart. My mother spoke up, and the answer remained the same, Ted later told me. "Heart attack," my mother had answered distinctly. Not even the hospital administrator was allowed to know how her father had died. She wouldn't say that unspeakable word, "suicide," to anyone, including her best friend Ina. After Danny's funeral when the rest of the family was talking about my grandfather's suicide, and how maybe there was a pattern, Ina came to me in tears. "Your mother is my best friend," she said. "How could she have never told me that her father killed himself?" I don't know whether it was a consolation or not but I tried to explain that it was something that my mother just wouldn't talk about, that she'd kept it a secret from me, too, until I finally discovered it for myself.

I found out the truth about my grandfather's death when my cousin Jon one day off-handedly referred to my grandfather's being found dead in the men's baths on the Lower East Side. I was dumbfounded. "What was he doing *there*?" I asked. Jon couldn't believe I knew nothing about our grandfather's death. It turned out that he had signed in at the baths not in his own name, but under the identity of Aunt Cecile's father-in-law. When the police called my aunt to report the death, he told her it was Stu's father who had just died in the baths. My cousin couldn't answer all of my questions—whether they'd actually found him floating in the water, or sitting somewhere near the edge. But what his mother, Cecile, had told him years ago was that our grandfather had taken a lot of pills and he was on the premises of the baths when they found him.

All of a sudden, the story was there. And by inheritance, it was my story, too. Despite my relentless questioning about my grandfather's death, I would never have come up with anything like this. And I was flooded with new feelings for my mother. I now understood that she had lived through a nightmare and why she wanted to run away from it. At the same time, I now had the proof that I'd been grasping for since birth. My mother had lied. As I'd always suspected, the world of enforced normalcy had been false. The "more" that I had always wanted was finally unfurling.

"How could you never have told me the truth?" I confronted her. Although I now felt a little heartless in my interrogation. "How could you not think this would affect my understanding of my own family and who I am?"

"He was *my* father," was what she said back. "What does it matter to *you*?"

My knowing the truth did nothing to change my mother. Her words were still unyielding, depriving me of any right to possess what had happened. And mostly, the rest of the world remained on her side. "That generation just didn't talk about suicide," people would say. "It was considered too shameful at the time. Don't be so hard on your mother." But finally I did have evidence. And I could now say with more certainty that regardless of how others might perceive my mother, that she had been hard on *me*.

I went to my aunt Cecile to find out more. Cecile was only two years younger than my mother, but she was completely different from her. The two of them came from the same generation and they had the same father, but my aunt told the truth. She was more like me. My mother must have thought so, too, because a lot of times she'd slip and call me "Cecile" by mistake.

I did know from my mother that she and Cecile used to fight fiercely when they were girls and had to share the same room. They stole each other's clothes. My mother would tell me in a competitive voice that Cecile was the "pudgy" one, while my mother was taller and thinner. I found out from Cecile that my mother's family nickname was "activity puss" because she was always running around keeping busy. When their mother was dying of breast cancer, Cecile told me, she and Joe tended to her on a daily basis, feeding her and changing her bandages, while my mother was never at home. Even though my mother and Cecile were sisters and had purportedly grown out of their childhood competitiveness, there was still a streak of jealousy that I could detect in my mother when it came to Cecile, who even though she was the younger one was the one who had married first, after falling madly in love with Stu at summer camp. My mother didn't get married until she was twenty-three, which even she said was considered to be late in those days.

Once I moved to New York, Cecile became my surrogate mother, or at least a great confidante. Also, she was a psychotherapist, and unlike my real mother was interested in seeking out answers. When I got to the point of such great anger with my mother that it was almost the only subject I could talk about, Cecile was the one who said, "And what are you going to do about that?" And those words were eventually what got me to a therapist's office, to begin a path of my own inquiry.

From my aunt, I found out that they'd grown up with the ever-present threat of their father's suicide. Two times during their childhood, my grandfather had tried to kill himself by putting his head in the oven. And on the second attempt, they had to call off the family's move to a new apartment in the Bronx. Instead they stayed on in the top floor of the brownstone on East 89th Street, where they lived with the whole extended family—my great-grandmother, great-grandfather, great-aunts and uncles living on the main two floors of the house, where they could all now keep a more careful eye on my grandfather. Protecting their own, they cushioned my grandmother Anna, who by then, Cecile told me, was sinking into her own depression, as she raised her family of four young children. I'd always wondered about the reverence my mother, Cecile, Joe, and Nate all had for my great-aunts and uncles, who seemed relatively removed from my world, and now there was an explanation for this.

From what Cecile told me, the unspoken consensus was that my grandfather Abe's side was the brash side of the family, ostentatious and overly preoccupied with money, not serious and Talmudic, like my grandmother's side. I knew that my grandfather was supposed to have been dashing, and had even heard him described as a "lady's man." But that was as far as anyone seemed to go in talking about my grandfather's unreliability. I knew from my mother and her siblings that they loved going to the beach in Far Rockaway during the summers, where my grandfather's side of the family lived, but they also laughed about this branch of the family. I'd heard of Aunt Esther's meticulously polished white floors, and how she wouldn't let anyone sit on the finely upholstered furniture. I imagined the women all wearing eyeglasses studded with rhinestones and playing mahjong on the beach, while the men played cards inside and chomped on cigars. But in truth I had no idea what they looked like because I'd never met them. Occasionally I'd heard their names in chatter between Cecile and my mother, but for the most part they were all but forgotten, even though they were in fact immediate family.

My grandfather's moods fluctuated a lot, Cecile told me. Sometimes he'd take my mother and Cecile on shopping sprees and buy them beautiful dresses before the Jewish holidays, or for no particular occasion at all. Their mother, Cecile said, would always stay at home. Other times, their father would run out of money, usually after a big argument with one of his partners in the liquor store or the dry goods business. But he was resourceful, and usually he'd spring back. Once, after my grandmother died, when my grandfather, his new wife, and Nate, who was still small, were living in a new neighborhood with no suitable school for Nate to attend, my grandfather, together with some partners, founded a progressive Jewish school of his own, so that his son would have a place to go to school. From what I could understand from Cecile, my grandfather was dark, handsome, and charming, and even though he could be inconsistent, he mainly made enough money to keep them comfortably middle class, and usually managed to hold his own with the more righteous side of the family. Eventually they did leave the family brownstone on East 89th Street and moved to the Bronx. Cecile was certain that my grandfather would have been diagnosed as "manic depressive" had the term existed during his lifetime.

The summer when we learned the truth about my grandfather, Ted and Danny were both living in Seattle. Ted was there for the year before starting medical school, and Danny was staying with him after just finishing his first year at Brown. When I went to visit them for a week and brought with me the astonishing news about our grandfather, Ted and I savored the new knowledge. We talked about it for hours—retracing the past, looking for signs that might have tipped us off beforehand and analyzing what this new realization might mean for us. We wondered whether there might be other cases of manic depression in the family, and whether anyone else had committed suicide in prior generations when they were still in Eastern Europe. But if anyone knew, or if anyone would talk about it, they would have to be on our grandfather's side of the family. And those were people we'd barely heard of, let alone try to ask them about family history. While Cecile, Joe, and Nate were more forthcoming about the past than my mother, they didn't consider her silence to be completely out of proportion. Nobody in generations past seemed to want to claim the volatile nature of our grandfather.

Danny, while Ted and I debated the new revelation in our lives, took no part on the topic of my grandfather. He was so quiet that I noticed it. Only later, after Danny died, did it occur to me that suicide might have been something he wanted to keep for himself, that he didn't want anyone to steal it from him even by talking about it. While Ted and I were speculating about our family and whether suicide might again strike, Danny may have already known more than we did. Ted later told me that when Danny had visited him in the hospital that summer of the recurrence of his kidney disease, he'd said something that had haunted Ted ever since. When he'd seen Ted lying in his hospital bed all hooked up to the IV's, he'd clearly said, "*No*, that's not fair! Now I can't die *first*." Ted hadn't known what to make of that, especially with my parents hovering around him—my mother overwhelmed with anxiety and my father infuriatingly optimistic about Ted's serious condition. But Danny's words stuck with him, especially when he remembered them later, after Danny killed himself.

That summer when we learned the truth about my grandfather, Ted and I both vowed we would never seal off unwanted secrets in our own lives. My mother may have been continuing an unspoken family campaign of not mentioning what she preferred not to have existed. But clearly neither her silence, nor her determined will to keep our lives in order, could stop the presence of my grandfather's legacy. We had all seeped it up, each in our own way, me fighting to know the truth, Ted more quietly striving to maintain a sense of stability, and Danny ultimately taking the damage on himself.

$$\approx$$

"It's Papa Joel," Eli says gleefully. He's jumped out of bed to answer the ringing phone. Eva wakes up, too, and joins in. "And Grandma Lois," she cries out.

"Grandma Lois, Grandma Lois," Eva parrots herself in a singsong-y voice.

She stops for a moment and looks at me thoughtfully. "Where is my grandma Lois?" she asks before answering her own question. "I lost her," she says.

Before leaving on their long trip to Australia and New Zealand, my mother had measured the length of Eva's arm one last time, to be sure she had the size just right before completing the sweater for her. If my mother had one art form, it was knitting. Her needles—metal, plastic, thick, thin, circular, whatever the pattern called for—were always clicking and kept her in motion. The profusion of sweaters, blankets, even dresses, could be seen as an indication of her good intent. Even at our most fractious times, my mother would usually have a sweater for me somewhere in the works. "Cardigan or pullover, which do you prefer?" There would be a book of patterns to consider, a yarn color or neckline to select. A week after I saw my mother for the last time, the new blue-green sweater, almost the exact color of Eva's eyes, came neatly packaged in the mail. She must have sent it off just as she left on her trip, and it reached us just as my parents were landing in New Zealand. Maybe if I keep reminding Eva that Grandma Lois made her this sweater, Eva will keep on asking about her. After spending so much of my life trying to detach myself from my mother, it's now become urgent to keep her spirit alive, or at least alive for my children.

My father is calling to confirm what time we plan to arrive in Andover. This weekend will be our first trip back since my mother's funeral. "With the Fourth of July traffic, you can never tell," I warn him. "But maybe we'll be there in time for lunch." He says he already has cheerios left from our last visit, and he'll go out to the store to get whatever else we need. I wonder if the kids will notice the cheerios being stale. "Pasta, cheddar cheese, bagels, milk, and orange juice," I list off the staples.

We arrive early and my father's face lights up when he sees us at the door. As we drag our suitcases into the house, I see him pull out a wrinkled plastic tablecloth, to set the table on the screened porch. He lifts a broom to knock down some cobwebs from the corners of the ceiling. Clearly, he hasn't yet used the porch this season.

Opening the refrigerator, I see the folly of having arrived without eating first. Sitting on the wire shelves are the relics that look like they've been there since the funeral last March. There's a small chunk of unused butter that's turned bright yellow, and some outdated containers of yogurt. I find a stub of cheddar cheese covered with mold and whittle it down, salvaging enough for a meal of pasta and cheese for the kids.

My father hauls a gallon of frozen milk up from the basement freezer. "I guess I'd better defrost this," he calls out. Living on his own, freezing the milk is something he's added to his oddball systems. He also now reuses garbage bags. He empties the contents of the plastic bag he keeps hanging under the sink daily, into the big barrel in the garage, he explains. He can then reuse the same plastic bag until the end of the week, when he throws the whole thing away. "On my own," he says, "there's not all that much garbage to take care of."

"Help yourself to whatever you'd like," he offers, like there's a wealth of food to choose from. I settle on a piece of toast with some hummus that has a relatively recent date on its container. Roy puts back the jar of jam when he notices that it's crystallized, and opts for a plain peanut butter sandwich. I try to clean out the refrigerator—the expired yogurt, a container of leftover soup that smells bad, and a couple of over-ripe peaches. My father always acted like he was the one who attended to getting rid of the leftovers, but it's clear that when it came to keeping things clean and aired out, my mother was in charge.

Except for the musty smell of the house and the state of the refrigerator, it's as if my mother is still here. Her clothes are all hanging where they used to be, although my father has bunched them together at one end of the closet. I rummage through her drawers, quickly at first, like I did when I was a little girl, afraid I'd be caught spilling a bottle of perfume or leaving an emerald ring or a bracelet in the wrong box by mistake. But then it occurs to me that I'm not really looking for anything. Most of my mother's jewelry was stolen years ago. Not a serious crime, just a scheme of a clever robber, who must have identified my mother's name listed in the *Andover Townsman*, announcing the time of her talk at the town library, a panel on ecumenical relations, scheduled to begin at five o'clock in the afternoon. Except for the missing jewelry and my mother's cherished silver candlesticks that had been a gift from my uncle Joe from the summer when he lived with us during law school, there wasn't any real damage. But gone forever were the sapphire and emerald rings made by my grandfather, my father's father who had been a jeweler. I was lucky I still had the bracelet of tiny pearls and rubies that my grandfather made for me before he died, when I was still a baby. All I can now find in my mother's drawer is a small collection of unfamiliar cardboard boxes with random trinkets inside. There are a couple of filigree Arab palms, probably gifts from admiring students and parents, and a pair of turquoise earrings I had brought back from a trip to Santa Fe. The pendants, Egyptian and Chinese replicas, must have been gifts that my father had bought at the Museum of Fine Arts. There's really nothing that seems like a treasure.

That evening, my father takes out the souvenir photo of himself and my mother on the cruise ship. The corners are bent, like he's looked at it a lot. He wants to show it to Eli and Eva.

"How old is Grandma?" asks Eli when my father shows him the picture. Eli has been asking this question about my mother's age repeatedly since she died.

"Sixty-eight," we all answer in unison.

"But how old is she now?" he asks again.

"Sixty-eight," I say back.

"She would be sixty-nine," my father says quietly, remembering that my mother's birthday had been in May.

"Is that how old she is she *now*?" Eli is insistent.

"Yes, she's sixty-nine," I finally say. And this seems to be the right answer.

The next day, we all meet at the beach—us, Ted, Janet, and the kids. My father leads the sandcastle building, but not as energetically as he used to. I keep on looking around, still not quite believing that my mother's not here as her grandchildren splash in the waves. On the way back we stop at our favorite homemade ice cream stand, and I can swear she's sitting right next to me, about to eagerly bite into her ice cream cone.

I sit with my father in the front seat, and he tells me stories about our life when we lived in Marblehead, stories about work. "What were the names of the other chemists, again?" I ask him. I'd completely forgotten about the Coleman brothers who owned the plastics company. Adrian was the older one, and Bobby was a fancy dresser who drove around in a convertible. I can easily remember my father's friend Austin who was gruff and whose jagged brown hair was always parted on the side.

Jack was the one we knew best. He looked older than my father, more like a grandfather, and every day he would drive my father home in his shiny black car. During the summer, Teddy and I would sit on the curb of the big main street, watching the cars go by until Jack's car would pull up and drop off my father. Then we'd all go home to eat supper, which my mother always had ready at six o'clock.

My father gets animated when he recounts the days when he and Jack teamed up to start their own company. "I was working at half the salary I made with the Colemans," he says. "And Jack worked for nothing. But then your mother and I decided we couldn't wait any longer for the business to take off. You kids were getting older, and it was too risky, so I had to leave Jack on his own." I already knew that a few years later Jack's business was thriving, although my father doesn't mention that.

It occurs to me that when we moved to Connecticut for my father's new job, it wasn't just leaving behind Marblehead that made life lose its spark. It was the time when my father must also have parted with some of his dreams. In the Connecticut job, my father had to drive almost an hour to get to work each day because we'd chosen a place to live in a suburb of Hartford where the schools were good. All I knew was that he'd bring us home samples from work—not just the wooden mixing sticks and glue like he used to, but now he brought bones that were actually plastic, but that looked real. Eventually we had the makings of almost an entire skeleton. He also worked on inventing plastic soda bottles, which at least seemed more exciting than the "polymers" he talked about at his old job.

Under the surface, I did have the unnamable sense that things were beginning to deteriorate when we lived in Connecticut. My mother whispered a lot in those years, especially when she thought we were asleep. I'd hear her talk too loudly about my father's boss whom he didn't seem to like very much. "What will you do next, Joel?" she'd say in a worried voice. "Is there another job you could get closer to Hartford?"

And sometimes my mother would talk quietly on the phone to Aunt Cecile about Uncle Joe, who might have to go to the hospital again. "It's a kind of sickness that's hard to explain," she'd say when I overheard her and asked what was wrong with Joe. She'd said to Cecile that in some ways it was a good thing that we'd moved to Connecticut because now we could be closer to Joe in case of emergency. The few times when my mother had to visit Joe, when he did have to go to the hospital, it was last minute and she'd have to apologize to the principal at the Hebrew school where she taught three days a week. Her friend Ruth would take over her classes when she went to visit Uncle Joe in Washington. My mother once told me that there weren't many good friends out there, but that Ruth was a really good friend. "Of course, I'll take over the classes," Ruth told her. "That's what good friends are for." Except for my father, I don't think my mother told anyone except for Ruth what was actually wrong with Uncle Joe. And it seemed like a big relief to her that Ruth understood whatever it was that she told her.

When we moved to Connecticut, Teddy was already taking large doses of prednisone, and his body was all puffed up. I felt bad for him because no one in our new school even knew he was actually a skinny kid. My mother tried to make us all eat "salt substitute" because Teddy couldn't have real salt because of his kidney disease. But really it was a bitter powder that tasted nothing like salt. And after a couple of weeks, we went back to real salt because Danny and I refused to eat our food, even though Teddy had to keep up with the salt substitute, although he said he didn't mind it. He'd make it seem like there was nothing to be scared of, even though he had to take a lot of medicine. He'd swallow ten or more different pills at a time—a whole multi-colored fistful at breakfast and another one at supper—all in one gulp.

In Connecticut I really hated going to Hebrew school. I had to be a grade ahead because the curriculum in Marblehead had been more advanced. And on top of that I had to go to bat mitzvah lessons. Even though my mother said it wasn't really important for girls to be bat mitzvahed, everyone in the school seemed to have one, so I had to have one, too. And I couldn't say no.

When I got home from school that Thursday afternoon before my bat mitzvah, my mother was in a flurry, wiping down the counters and scouring the burners of the stove. "This entire place is sticky from those damned *French tuiles*," she said in disgust. "You won't have to remind me never to make those again. What a pain!" My mother's plan was to have the reception at the house after the Friday night service, and she'd make all the pastries. Even if it took the whole week, she wanted to do it herself. She'd gotten the French tuile recipe from her friend Velma, the best baker she knew. There were plates of the tuiles covering the counters and the table—delicate tube-shaped cookies with colored frosting coated with sugar at the ends. Even though I knew a big part of my mother's aim was to get praise for creating these elaborate things, I still wanted to believe that she was making them for me. And they really were pretty. But now she said the whole baking effort hadn't been worth it. The bat mitzvah turned out to be another chore, just like I knew it would be.

It was around then when my mother said she was worried about Danny because she didn't think he had enough confidence. He was six or seven at the time, and he seemed perfectly happy to me. "You have to give him more of a chance to speak at supper," she told Teddy and me one night after Danny had left the table. "It's starting to affect his self-confidence the way you cut him off all the time." I remember being surprised that my mother spoke about Danny, or anyone else for that matter, in that way. But still, it seemed ridiculous. The reason we didn't let him speak was because at that age he was too young to really have much to contribute to the conversation, I thought at the time. But when I think about it now, I can barely remember Danny from the time when we lived in Connecticut. I wonder what life had been like for him in those colorless years.

I remember riding in the back seat of the station wagon, and tickling him until he cried with laughter. And he would tickle me back, and get me laughing hysterically, too. "Don't stoop to his level!" my mother would yell at me. But I didn't care about her insults. Danny was my playful companion, and I was his protector. My mother was just mean. I would take care of myself, and Danny, too.

When Danny was in high school and I was visiting from college, I was in charge of taking him to see some college campuses. After his interview at Wesleyan, we realized that I'd locked the keys in the car. We could see them through the car window, right there in the ignition. We were parked in front of a dry cleaner, and it was Danny's idea to ask inside for a wire hanger. I unbent it, managed to pry it through the top of the window, and finally looped the hanger around the inside handle and opened the door. I knew I hadn't exactly taken on the adult role, but we had fun together, and I was sure it had to be better than going around visiting colleges with my parents.

My parents thought that maybe Danny could help *me* when I was moving my stuff back from Chicago after a year in graduate school. So they paid for his plane ticket to fly out to meet me. I'd rented a Ryder truck, and Danny was supposed to share the driving. I wasn't at all surprised when he just lazed around, while I wrapped up all of my dishes, pots, and pans, and put all the books into boxes. But still it was a comfort just to see him sitting there. Once we had everything loaded into the back of the truck, and slammed the doors shut, we climbed onto the front seats that were high off the ground. Danny was going to drive first. Then we noticed the sign on the dashboard saying that you had to be twenty-one years old to drive the vehicle. Danny had just turned eighteen a few weeks before and we didn't want to take any chances, so we switched and I took the driver's seat. We began jerking along the Hyde Park streets, while I tried to get the truck into gear. "Careful!" Danny would say, laughing and pretending to duck his head as I hit some low-hanging branches. Finally we made it to the highway, and began to relax. After an hour or so, the radio on loud, Danny pointed out a sign that said we were entering Wisconsin. Danny pulled out the map to be sure we were going in the right direction, and in fact we'd been driving west rather than east. We had just added two hours to our trip, and we had only just started. We laughed as I maneuvered the exit and turned us around. Eventually, we arrived in Andover, me driving the truck the entire time. But Danny kept me laughing, and it seemed like we needed each other to make it the whole way.

"Mom, how old will you be when I'm 100?" Eli asks. We're on our way back to New York, crossing into Connecticut from the Mass Pike.

"139," I answer.

"Will you be dead?" Eli asks.

"Probably. I don't know for sure, but most people don't live that long. 139 is very old."

"When we go to Maine this summer, Papa Joel will visit us, right?" Eli asks.

"And Grandma Lois?" Eva adds.

"No, she won't be there. She went away," I say, trying to keep things simple.

"She went a type of 'away' that's called *die*," Eli tells her. "I wonder what happened to Grandma Lois," he says with a slight push in his voice.

"Well, you know that she's buried, right?" I reply.

"Yes, but what *happened* to her?"

"She was old." I know this answer is no longer sufficient. "And sometimes when people are old, their bodies stop working. Grandma's body stopped working."

"And it hurt her a lot," he presses again.

He wants the truth. The last thing I want to do is to not tell him. But still I don't know what to say. I don't know if her heart really just stopped, or if she died of fear, or if maybe she was stung by a poisonous fish. I don't even know how to remember her—how to hold onto her spirit, or how to admit what it was really like to have her for a mother.

"It didn't necessarily hurt," I say.

Five

The house we're renting this August in Deer Isle really is round. It's a gray wooden structure, sitting up high on stilts, and it has windows all around facing the ocean. Besides that, the first thing I notice is the deck with a wide-open railing that wraps all the way around the house. Right away I can imagine Eva walking right through it and falling into the bushes below.

"Back in the car," says Roy. We've just driven nine hours to the very end of this long dirt road that juts way out into the ocean. But before going any further, we have to do something about the big, gaping deck.

We get back into the car, and drive straight to the hardware store. We know just where to go because we came to Deer Isle last August, too, but last year we'd stayed in a different house that we shared part of the time with another family. Slamming the car door in the Burnt Cove parking lot, I yell out to Roy, "Let's pick up some eggs, milk, and juice while we're here!" But Roy says, "No, for now let's just go to the hardware store." He just wants to get the problem solved. We find some bright yellow rope and buy all three packages that are on the shelf, and then lug them back to the car. "Now can we go home to our round house?" asks Eli. The kids can't stand being in the car anymore, and who can blame them. Back we go, out to the very end of the long dirt road again, back to our house.

Armed with our bright yellow rope, this time we open the door of our new home and look around. There's a nice, open kitchen with bright blue countertops. And the living room looks out onto the far-reaching water. Right in the center of the house is a spiral staircase that leads down to the bedrooms. I envision more dangerous tumbles to the ground.

Roy unwinds the yellow rope, and together we weave it and tie it all the way around the deck railing, making a bright web of prevention that looks like a construction site. When that's finished, we use the remaining piece of rope inside on the spiral staircase, zigzagging it back and forth through the spokes and around the banister.

Where I am prone to being fearful and ready to plunge into the past, Roy is practical and very much in the here and now. He jokes about my always needing to have a good supply of toilet paper, dishwashing soap, olive oil, and mustard. "We live in a city," he says. "We don't need to have a storeroom. We can buy things when we need them." It's the same when I want to have tools on hand, and nails, screws, and scotch tape in case something breaks. "That's why we have a super," he says. "That's why we live in an apartment building." It's taken me years to understand that Roy doesn't need to prepare for all kinds of material eventualities. The fact is that he's already taken care of the larger issues, like life insurance policies and health care plans, and he's basically confident about the world. When the railing needs to be fixed, he's rational about figuring out how to do it. He doesn't get held up thinking about what might go wrong.

When I first met Roy's family, I was impressed to discover that his mother always carried a measuring tape in her pocket book, ready to calculate the dimensions of any table or chair she might want to buy at a flea market, or to accurately judge whether a particular pot or pan would fit properly on a shelf. Roy's whole family is like that, very keyed into the details. They're all good at reading floor plans for apartments, something I can never really fathom until the actual space is in front of me and fully arranged with furniture.

The plan is for me and the kids to be out here for the whole month. Roy's set aside these couple of days to help us settle into the house before he drives back to New York. Tomorrow we'll pick up a rental car in Bangor for us to use until Roy returns again. August is when things start to get busy for him at work, so he can't take that much time off. He's spent his whole career as a lawyer dedicated to educational policy. Now he works in a university system, so there's a lot of administrative planning and politics to handle before the school year begins. But he'll get back up here for at least a week at the end of the month.

This month in Deer Isle is the refuge I've been waiting for. It's the big break from the everyday confusion of work and the kids' school and babysitting schedules. I've spent weeks getting organized, tying up loose ends in my office, paying all the bills ahead of time, gathering all the things we'll need up here—sunscreen and insect repellant, organic fruit snacks for Eli's camp lunches, and birthday presents for Eva, who will be turning two in just a couple of weeks. Maybe now that we're finally here I'll have the time to really think about my mother.

We've made the kids' beds, unpacked our clothes into the drawers, and put some food in the cabinets, and now it's time to take a walk to the beach. Down the rickety steps we go. The round granite rocks crunch under our sandals as we make our way to the water. A big dragonfly lands on Eli's arm. "Mom, what do I do?" he shrieks.

"Just brush it off," I shout back, laughing a little to myself at how my city kids need to adjust to life in the wilds. But at the same time I'm wondering how I'll ever manage here by myself without the trappings of my everyday city routine.

The first night that Roy's gone, I'm quaking in the silent darkness. There are rustling noises coming from the woods in the back, and I ask myself whether there might be animals or people out there. For some reason, animals seem less frightening because I don't think they'll come inside. I remind myself that I'm the mother, that I'm the one watching over my children who are sleeping peacefully in the room next to mine.

Morning is a big relief. Not only is the night over, but it's a beautiful day. And it's Eli's first day of camp. The three of us get into the car, and I follow the directions on the brochure that tells us where we're going. From the parking lot, there's a dirt path into the woods. Eli bounds ahead, first to the arts and crafts shed and then down to the waterfront and boating house. Eli is one of the youngest, but he seems to be making a friend right away, so I quickly say goodbye, thinking he'll be fine in this lovely old-fashioned world. Eva and I return to the house to meet up with the babysitter, the sister of the girl who helped out with the kids last summer. I'm impressed that the babysitter has brought her own books to read to Eva, and I leave the two of them reading *Madeline* on the front steps and wave goodbye.

This is my life in Maine, I tell myself. Monday is dump day, so I begin by taking the garbage to the dump. Next I set out to try to find a vegetable stand that I vaguely remember from last summer. It's a couple of towns over, and like everything else here it's a twenty or thirty minute drive away. As I navigate the road and try to recall which turn is the right one, it comes back to me that when I first found this stand last August, I had been sitting in the car with my mother. It was when my parents were visiting us for a few days in Maine. Remarkably I again find the stand, just a small wooden structure by the side of the road with a farm in the back. I pick out a few great-looking, ripe tomatoes and a nice bag of green beans, and get back in the car feeling like I've accomplished something. There I am, driving home alone at last with my vegetables beside me on the seat. All of the tension lets loose and I cry all the way back to the round house.

We develop our routine. I get Eli to camp on time in the morning, leave Eva to play with the babysitter so that I can do work—make phone calls and answer the mail that's been forwarded from my office to the local post office—and then I move on to my errands. Monday, Tuesday, and Thursday, after taking the garbage to the dump, I head for the grocery store. Friday is the Deer Isle Farmers' Market. Sometimes I check out a gallery, or see if there's a new pair of earrings at the jewelry store in Deer Isle Center, which is really no more than a crossroads. If there's enough time and it's a warm enough day, I try to go for a swim in the Lily Pond. In the late afternoon, Eva and I pick up Eli at camp, and usually we all go back to the pond again to swim. Actually, they play in the water and I watch them. In the evening, I get the grill lit, bathe the kids while the charcoals are getting hot, get the chicken or hotdogs cooking (I've given up encouraging them to eat fish even though we're in Maine), and try to keep an eye on the grill while also watching to be sure Eva doesn't run down to the water by herself. The kids bicker over who gets the blue washcloth and who gets the green one. And at dinner they both want to sit on the same side of the table as me. "You have to learn to take turns," I tell them an uncountable number of times. I bribe them. "If everyone cooperates, we all get to eat our dessert on the beach." And then we go out to the rocks with our ice cream sandwiches.

It's an intense little world we dwell in. And part of what fortifies us is that we're in it together, just me and Eli and Eva in a phenomenally beautiful environment. Once it's dark and they're completely asleep downstairs in their bedroom at the bottom of the spiral staircase, I quietly make my way back upstairs. I lean back into the pillows of the living room couch and marvel as I look around. The big, curved window that looks out on the water is actually a series of panes. With the lights on inside, and the darkness outside, each pane reflects the moon, so it looks like there are eight moons, each shining on a piece of illuminated water.

As the days pass I have more time to swim and dry off in the sun, and even gain enough attention to read a few chapters of a book. Slowly, the air, the trees, and the gentle beauty begin to slip under my skin. And even deeper than that, I can feel my muscles start to relax. I watch Eli and Eva scamper around on the deck. Eva runs inside to change into different bathing suits, returning back to model them, and Eli makes guns out of sticks. Maybe soon my mind will clear, and I'll have the time to really think about what it means that my mother has died.

On the day of her second birthday, Eva wakes up at 5:30 a.m. I bring her into bed with me, to try to get her to go back to sleep. It was right around this time two years ago when I was having early labor pains and she was about to be born. She hugs me and sings snippets of different rhyming songs. And eventually she falls back asleep. I get out of bed to do the sun salutations that I try to do most mornings, something I started doing a few months after Eva was born. Then I get back into bed and doze off beside Eva before the day begins.

When she wakes up the second time, she's ready to celebrate. She loves her presents—blow-up toys for the water, and a new bathing suit. We take Eli to camp, and come home to make her cake. In the afternoon the two of us sit by the water and play with stones on the beach, just holding them, turning them over in our hands and feeling their warmth. We throw our stones into the water and watch the splashes they make. At night we all sing "Happy Birthday, and Eva blows out the candles.

When Roy returns to spend the last week with us, immediately I sleep more peacefully. The broken dreams that I've been having about my mother and Danny stop right away. The one about Danny is a variation on a recurring theme—he's still alive and he's only been wandering around for years, never really dead. He tells me about his journeys and beckons me to come with him, but then drifts away again and I wake up feeling tortured by the reality.

A couple of nights ago, I had a beautiful dream about my mother. I was lost on the way to school in the first grade. I was walking on a street in a town very unlike my own, cold, with brick buildings reminiscent of small, austere towns in upstate New York. The name of the town was "Hydro." I roamed past an old, brick power plant. I turned a corner and walked up the stairs to my house and rang the bell. A woman who was my mother answered the door wearing a diaphanous dress in a pale shade of greenish blue. Apparently she and I lived there alone. In my dream, I kept waking up and knowing that the woman wasn't really my mother, but then I'd keep on going back to sleep again so I could be with her.

My father pays us a visit, and here in this beautiful setting, he seems especially sad. His dark eyes look sunken into his nicely shaped bald head that's covered with faded freckles. Insistent on shielding himself from the sun, he sometimes even wears his baseball cap inside. His skin looks a little gray, not the healthy kind of tan color he usually is this time of year.

Last year, when my father and mother came together to visit us in Deer Isle, he ran around with Eli teaching him how to fly a kite. And my mother made pies with the Maine blueberries. My father says he's been keeping active, playing tennis and riding his bike sometimes. He tells me he's even gone out on a couple of dates. He's especially impressed by one woman who's recently learned to play the cello. "Maybe I could try to learn to play a musical instrument, too," he says. "Maybe the violin." He briefly mentions a woman named Judith Taylor. I've heard of her before. She and her husband used to play duplicate bridge sometimes with my parents, and I know that Judith's husband had died right around the same time as my mother. My father says they've gone out to dinner a couple of times and once to see a movie. "Really?" I ask. "Is she nice?" But he doesn't appear to be interested in my question. It seems difficult for him to stay focused on anything. It's as though all of his senses are dulled, not just his hearing. He's forgotten to bring his bathing suit, so he can't go swimming. And he didn't remember his sunscreen. When I offer him mine, he says it's not a high enough SPF number. It won't protect him enough.

Most striking is his loss of capacity to play with Eli and Eva.

"Come into the water with me, Papa Joel," says Eli, taking off his sandals at the edge of the Lily Pond.

"No, I can't," says my father, his shoes tied, his dark socks pulled up to his calves.

"He forgot his bathing suit," I say. "He'll watch you from the blanket."

"Come on, Papa Joel," says Eli.

My father doesn't even walk down to the water.

"I'll come in with you," says Roy, who's usually not very interested in playing in the water.

I wonder whether my father will now be sad forever. After Danny died, his dreams were completely shattered. Maybe my mother's death on top of that will be more than he can take.

"Danny's gone," were my father's words that night when he called to tell me that Danny had died. For a moment, I didn't understand what he was trying to say. Was he saying that Danny had left on a trip? But then immediately I knew. "How did he do it?" I asked. I don't think he could have possibly answered me. I don't remember exactly who told me how Danny had killed himself, that he had cut his abdomen with a kitchen knife in the restaurant where he worked.

I screamed when I heard what happened, and must have woken up my apartment mate, someone I hardly knew. But she didn't come into my room. I'd moved into that apartment a couple of months before when I'd left my job at the auction house. I was now relying on the small income I could get from freelance work before starting my new job as an editorial assistant at a publishing house in the fall, and I couldn't afford my own place anymore. "What are you doing in there?" my new roommate would periodically open the door of my bedroom and try to engage me in conversation or try to share a bowl of the popcorn that she made with her special air popper that didn't use any fat. "Why are you always *reading*?" she'd ask. She thought all the books I'd unpacked into the living room shelves made the place look messy. My bedroom was where I'd sit doing my freelance copyediting jobs and commenting on manuscripts for movie companies, trying to make enough money to pay the rent. Occasionally I'd leave to go out to the park to run around the reservoir, something I hated, but forced myself to do anyway so I could get some exercise.

Something very terrible was brewing during those months before Danny died. I barely ate, and would burst into tears if I passed a homeless person on the street. Something as slight as a person walking away from me at a party because they said they wanted to get a drink would make me cry. There had been that succession of phone calls from Danny.

"That woman is a horror," he said about his boss who ran the restaurant where he worked in the kitchen. I couldn't understand it, but he really seemed to abhor that woman. "She really despises me," he'd say. "There must be something I can do to get back at her." He spoke with a kind of venom that made me nervous.

The last time he'd visited me the summer before he died we'd gotten into a screaming fight. It was the weekend of a big march against nuclear weapons, and Danny had come to New York for the protest. We had all walked together in the long procession, chanting, "No nukes!" Danny with me and my friends. There was music playing everywhere and Danny would periodically drift over to the side and dance by himself, sometimes closing his eyes. I worried that he seemed really alienated, but also I couldn't stand him. By then he was perpetually berating me for seeing the world wrong, and for the way I treated him. "You don't ever see me for who I am!" he'd accuse me. "I'm not a little kid. You can't even treat me like a real person." And he was right that I still thought of him more as my adorable brother. And that wasn't who he was anymore, not at all. The person he had become was exhausting. He didn't smell good, and his patchy beard made him look unappealing. He taunted me to the point that I physically tried to push him out of the apartment. That's how that last visit ended, I kicked him out.

In September, he called to say he'd be in New York for a Grateful Dead concert. Could he stay with me? he wanted to know. I'd barely spoken to him since that last miserable visit, and I was so thankful that I would see him again. He said he'd arrive sometime before dinner, but he never showed up. "Aren't you angry at him?" my roommate tried to commiserate as I cleared the table, including Danny's unused plate. But angry was the last thing I was. And when I burst into tears, my roommate stopped asking questions. A couple of days later, Danny called to say he'd decided not to stay that night, but had gone straight back to Providence.

One small part of me was a little relieved after Danny died. I was always frightened that the worst thing imaginable was going to happen, and then it did. The morning of the funeral, I remembered to call my therapist from my parents' house, to tell him I couldn't make it to our session because my brother had committed suicide. Like usual, he didn't say much back to me, but maybe this time it was because he was shocked. "Now that Danny is dead, I may not be coming back to therapy," I told him. "The worst is now over." In my state, I must have thought that Danny's death could be neatly consumed. Even though I couldn't have been more wrong about that, in some ways I was right about the worth of the therapy. I kept on seeing that therapist for another couple of years, but really I was too bereft to make any kind of progress.

Danny was in Providence when he died on October 13th. It was Wednesday night. He'd been brought to the hospital in an ambulance, and the police tried to reach Ted to tell him because that was the number they found first. When Ted wasn't home, the police found my father's phone number, and he was the one who called to tell me. My aunt Cecile called to say I should pack a bag. She and Stu were coming from Queens to pick me up, and we'd drive straight to Andover. "What else is there to do?" Cecile said. The sun was coming up as we got off the exit and turned onto Main Street. We were almost there, closer to the truth, closer to where Danny was. Maybe once I was there, I would know more.

Roy takes Eli down to the water, splashes him, and throws him in the air. Eva slaps around in the mud by their feet. Roy's eyes are the sparkly pale blue they get in the summer when he's a little tanned and near the water. His hair is light brown, and I can imagine it with blond streaks when he was little, just like Eva has. He's not tall, shorter than my side of the family, but not diminutive either. It's impossible not to be in the present with Roy's matter-of-fact personality. He's almost the opposite of my father, who often seems to be living in riddles.

Roy doesn't understand my father's logic, but that doesn't seem to bother him. He knows how to joke around with him in a way that I can't.

By the end of the month, I know we've all been softened by our time in Maine. It hasn't been the great opening up I'd imagined, more of a passing of time. I think we'll come back to Deer Isle again next summer, to this same round house so perfectly perched on the water. Maybe Roy will have less work, and he'll be able to spend more time with us. But first there is still a year to come in between. Eli will start kindergarten and Eva will begin her first year of preschool, and our schedules will take over. From this quiet spot in Maine, it doesn't seem too daunting.

Six

Great-Uncle Harry and Aunt Martha are old, but they've come up to Boston for my cousin Rachel's wedding. The last time I saw them was more than ten years ago at Joe's funeral, and I remember they looked really angry. Maybe they were demoralized over another family member tragically and irreligiously taking his own life. I barely talked to them, but then again I don't know them very well. They come from another generation. This time, though, they're beaming in a way I've never seen before. Rachel is marrying an observant Jew, and she's asked Harry and Martha's son David, our second cousin who's a rabbi, to officiate. Rachel circles seven times around her husband under the canopy while David says a blessing.

The wedding scene looks incomplete, like a tableau of the remains of our family. Uncle Joe, Aunt Cecile, and my mother are no longer here. Only Nate remains from his generation. With his dark eyes widely set, and his face tanned after the summer, he resembles the others. I've seen pictures of him as a child when his hair was blonde. There's always been something about him that seemed a little lighter than the rest of them, less troubled by what had happened over the course of growing up in their family. I know that Nate adores Uncle Harry and Aunt Martha. They do look like pillars of the family, sitting there smiling.

My mother was the one in her generation to carry the religious torch. Cecile said she couldn't wait to stop keeping kosher and started ordering Chinese take-out, including pork and shrimp, as soon as she was married and had a home of her own. Joe and Nate belonged to synagogues in Washington and their kids went to Hebrew school, but they didn't take it as seriously as my mother did. My mother kept two sets of dishes. And no matter where we lived, she'd find a good kosher butcher. When she baked a dessert for a meat meal, she always used margarine instead of butter. My mother's high school and college boyfriends had all been rabbinical students until she married my father. My father would comply by singing the *kiddush* on Friday nights, but he couldn't quite be depended upon to observe the rituals. He didn't have the conviction about being Jewish that my mother would have preferred. It was probably one of the things about him that annoyed her. Once when we were on vacation, my father ordered ham and yams in a restaurant. I was intrigued by that. "What are yams?" I remember asking. Once I had more independence, I happily followed his lead, ordering fried clams with my friends' families from the stand at the beach. When McDonald's first opened and we stopped there on the drive to New York, and my mother of course ordered the fish sandwich, I would be sure to ask for a cheeseburger. It was a pleasure to unwrap the greasy yellow paper and open up the bun to find the melted cheese and thin slices of pickle on top of the hamburger patty, all neatly packaged with ketchup and mustard, even though I didn't really like cheeseburgers.

Joe's funeral turned out to be on Easter Sunday. All the daffodils were out and the cherry blossoms were in full bloom in Washington. It was a warm and sunny day when we followed the hearse past the suburban neighborhoods and shopping malls on the way to the cemetery. As we drove by people wearing their brightly colored Easter clothes, Joe's death, and all of the death that seemed to be sunk into our family, felt out of place with the rest of the world.

Uncle Joe had been a kind of family patriarch. He took over the liquor store business when his father died, even though he was still only in college and also the editor of the school newspaper. After that he went to Harvard Law School, where he was on the Law Review. And he became a successful Washington lawyer and lived in a big house in the suburbs. I first learned what engraved printing was when we would periodically receive cream colored cards with raised black lettering, announcing Joe's new legal positions, and eventually the formation of his own firm. "Look at the new engraved card from Joe!" my mother would say whenever the latest one arrived. When he committed suicide some of his colleagues who attended the funeral couldn't believe it because he had been so capable and so successful.

Joe became especially interested in me and Ted after Danny died. And even before that, he generously paid for my therapy bills when I couldn't afford them. He'd take me out to fancy dinners whenever he came to New York. And he'd always bring the conversation around to what he referred to as the "history of violence" and the suicide that pervaded the family. It was true that I'd come to consider suicide as one of the ways you could potentially die—like cancer, a heart attack or dying in your sleep. And I knew that other people didn't necessarily think that way. But I couldn't quite understand Joe's compulsion to talk about the "violent tendencies" that he saw as inevitable in our family.

"I know our family has had suicides," I'd say. "But I don't really know what you mean by a history of violence," I'd urge him to explain. Then Joe would go on with the story about how his mother was so rough with him that she'd once yanked his arm too hard to keep him from falling down the stairs. The account had reached legendary proportion over the many years that he'd repeated it, to the point that he now said he'd been in excruciating pain when his mother had actually "pulled the arm out of its socket." Some of us even joked about how the story had grown. But Joe refused to be teased about it, even though he could sometimes be the first to laugh at his own jokes. The story held some deep significance for him, something I couldn't fully grasp.

The first time Joe had been hospitalized was the summer when he was in law school, when he'd come to stay with us. Of course I didn't know it then, but that was a time when he needed a familial roof over his head, and we lived in nearby Marblehead. I now also understood that when my mother made those trips to Washington when we lived in Connecticut, she'd met up with Cecile to visit Joe at a psychiatric facility, not the regular hospital where people went with heart attacks or broken bones. I now knew that it was a big accomplishment for Joe to have lived past fifty, the age his father was when he committed suicide. We'd all wondered whether Joe would survive that threshold. By then we had family conversations about the side effects that Joe sometimes had from the medication he took for depression, and how it could be difficult to get the dosage right.

We talked about how the term "manic depression" didn't exist yet when his father committed suicide. And how maybe that was part of the reason no one really talked about it in earlier generations, because there wasn't a name for it yet. I wondered whether Danny would have been called manic depressive had a diagnosis ever been made. I thought that with Danny's charismatic personality, and the way the symptoms hit suddenly in his early twenties, from what I'd read it might also have been schizophrenia. But according to Joe, he had to be manic depressive because that was what ran in our family. He said that almost like he owned it.

I still wonder whether Danny really had the genes that seemed to run in my mother's side of the family. Physically, he was the one who looked most like my father. And I didn't entirely trust Joe's comprehension of Danny. Even though they both eventually ended their own lives, with Joe suicide was a driving obsession. Danny, I still believe, might have gone a different way if only he'd had the chance to experience more of life. I wonder still what would have happened if Danny had been born a decade later when medication for depression was a more recognized part of the culture, and if that might have kept him alive. If he had lived, I wondered if he would always have suffered, and if I would have had to go to visit him in the hospital. Maybe he could have been treated, and eventually lived his life. Recently I happened to be with my father in a clothing store in my neighborhood on the Upper West Side, when a college friend of Danny's appeared. Immediately, he recognized my father's signature bald head, and came over to say hello to us. It took a few moments until I recognized Matt. He was with his adolescent daughter, buying a Mother's Day gift for his wife. My father was thrilled to see him, a link to his lost son. But I just stood there, trying to place exactly when I'd last seen Matt, and how old he must now be. What would Danny have been like, if he'd been almost forty like Matt must be now?

When I saw the movie *28 Up*, Michael Apted's documentary that follows the lives of a group of British children, filming them every seven years, I wept over the interview with the boy who seemed to be a lot like Danny. "Give me the child when he is seven, and I will show you the man," was the Jesuit quote that inspired the movie. In many of the cases that seemed to be true, but not for the character who reminded me most of Danny. That boy grew up to be a young man of twenty-eight in a mental institution. But then I continued to follow the series, and when I saw *35 Up* I was no longer sure whether that boy was like Danny or not. By thirty-five, the Danny character was out of the hospital and a functioning member of society. Ted says he's sure that Danny had a chemical illness, and if he'd ever survived, he would have had to live with the agony of it for his whole life. But there's always the lingering belief that it might not have been like that.

"Danny was so young," I found myself pleading with Joe. "Maybe if he could have just made it a few more years, he could have had a better sense of the order of life and maybe he would have survived."

"No," Joe said. "That's not possible. Once the pendulum starts swinging, it can't be stopped."

I wanted *Joe* to stop. I didn't want any more suicides, and with Joe I could never be sure. "How about seeing the light at the end of the tunnel?" I tried to change the metaphor. But it didn't work.

"When I look," Joe said, "I only see a tunnel. No light."

Joe was going to follow through with his death, and our family by now recognized the signs ahead of time. Almost methodically, he began to estrange those who loved him unconditionally. He abruptly rejected my aunt Helene, his wife of more than twenty-five years and the mother of his three children, my cousins who would have to bear the burden of his act. He moved out of the big, suburban house he had been so proud of, and into an apartment of his own. He began a vicious campaign of insults against my aunt Cecile, his sister and lifelong ally and confidante. It was impossible not to become embroiled in his plan. It was impossible to support him as he inflicted pain and anger on anyone who might have helped. We could see disaster approaching. And Joe was right, there was nothing we could do to stop him.

Even he himself was unable to interrupt his path. Recognizing his own danger, like he had before, he checked himself into a hospital. But this last time, he didn't or couldn't wait for the medication to kick in. Unheeded by nurses, he walked right out of the hospital doors, back to his newly rented apartment, where he sealed the doors and windows and turned on the oven and died, in the same way his father had twice tried to do.

After Joe died, we now had another suicide in our family ranks. It wasn't just the death itself this time, but the recurrence of it. With Joe's death we now had suicide in three consecutive generations. And my mother, as much as she had tried to avoid it, was right in the center of it, the surviving victim of father, son, and brother, all who had died by suicide. This had to qualify as a "history of violence."

I could now see that when I'd confronted my mother about her father's suicide, she was right to have claimed, "he was *my* father." It was much worse for her than it would ever be for me, one step removed. Being granddaughter, sister, and niece was a lot different from being daughter, mother, and sister. I felt the vibrations of the violence for sure, but still I had the notion that I could be free of the nets of death, that I could step forward and not have to run away like my mother did. What I could now identify as something of a family legacy made me take a deep breath, and when I did, it could literally hurt to consider it. But I could also see how the pattern might be something of the past, a past that included growing up under the auspices of my mother's fearful vision, but did not necessarily have to be part of my present and future. I was separate from my mother, after all. Maybe that had been the very point of my struggle with her. I was desperate for her love, but it was also a relief to be able to have things my way, not to have to be her.

After Rachel's wedding, Roy, Eli, Eva, and I drive up to Andover with my father. "I've been organizing your mother's things," he tells me, "just in case I decide to move out some day. Maybe I'll get a place closer to Boston."

"We need to go home tomorrow," I tell him. "But don't worry, I can come back to help you put Mom's things in boxes."

"No," he says. "I think I can handle that myself."

Before we leave he presses a small package into my hand. I unwrap the scotch tape and tissue, and open it to find my mother's engagement ring. "You should have it," he says.

When I get home, I unwrap the ring again and look at it carefully. The sparkling diamond, that had been set by my grandfather, reminds me of my mother's eyes and face. But I don't know exactly what to do with it. I wrap it up again, and put it in the back corner of my drawer.

Eli is getting more persistent about figuring out what could have possibly happened. "Did people see her die?" he asks. "Was anyone watching while she was dying?" Seven months have passed and I still haven't told him anything new.

"No, I don't think anyone was watching," I say.

"Did Papa Joel see her die?" he keeps on asking. "After she died, did people come to take her away?"

At the breakfast table, Eli taunts Eva. "You don't know where Grandma Lois is," he says.

"Yes, I do," Eva says in a playful voice. "She's at home."

"No she's not, she's *dead*." He says the final *d* with a thud.

"She's not dead."

"She is."

"She's not dead-ie," Eva begins to sing a little.

"She is dead."

"She's not dead-ie."

"She is dead-ie."

Eva has now started asking questions of her own, especially when I put her to sleep. "Do sheep die?" she asks me. "Do giraffes die? Do elephants die?" She tries to cover all the animals she can think of. "Yes," I tell her repeatedly, "when they get very old they die."

One night she asks, "Do ghosts die?" I'm surprised at the mysteriousness of her question. "Actually, ghosts don't die.

They're not real," I say. Meanwhile, Eli from his bed across the room tries to make Eva laugh. "Do watering cans die?" he asks. They both think this is hilarious. Only when Eva starts making funny bleating noises do I realize that she's asking me whether goats die, not ghosts.

I wonder what they already know, what they may have overheard and what they imagine. Possibly one of the cousins has said something to Eli, although I don't think so. I'm pretty sure he would have mentioned that. I ask myself yet again what I can tell him to help make some sense, and how much to tell him. And I still don't know the answers.

I'd been furious with Ted for pouncing with the news about telling his kids about my mother's death *and* Danny's all at once. But maybe there was more sense to it than I'd allowed. Whenever I find myself thinking about how I will someday talk to Eli and Eva about my mother's death, I'm better able to anticipate telling them about Danny, despite the harshness of those details, which are so much more overpowering. The core of my mother's death always seems to bring up Danny. During our last visit to my father, Eli noticed the photograph of Ted, Danny, and me as children, hanging on the den wall just like it always did. But this time, for the first time, Eli seemed to notice Danny. "Who's that?" he inquired about the photograph of my then two-year-old brother.

Long poised for this moment, I was ready with my answer. "When I was little," I said, "I had another brother besides Ted. His name was Danny."

But Eli didn't seem to be interested in Danny. "How old are you in that picture?" he asked, jumping back into the photograph and away from my words.

"About eight."

"But you're wearing a watch," he observes. "Can you wear a watch when you're eight?"

He wasn't yet ready for whatever news I might want to deliver about Danny. And still, I didn't know what I could possibly say about my mother.

≈

On Eli's second day of kindergarten, he comes home and announces that he's made his first new friend. "My friend is Michael," he says. "First we sat next to each other, then we held hands, and then we were friends," he tells me proudly. I secretly go into the bathroom and cry at his innocence as he begins his official school education.

All of my own first days of school in the fall rush back. No more of my mother's tanned and relaxed face at the beach, where we'd all been weathered by the salt water and sand over the months of the summer. The wild roses that we passed on our walk from the parking lot to the beach had lost most of their petals even though they still smelled sweet. It was during the summer when my mother was happiest, when she would sometimes join us in giddy, uncontrollable laughter, the kind that takes over for no particular reason when you're trying to be quiet in synagogue. At Rosh Hashanah services my mother would sometimes still have a little of the summer left in her. She wouldn't get angry when we started giggling, but would say, "shhh," with a slight smile, like she knew what it was like to be stuck in a laughing fit, too.

September is the month of Roy's birthday. As a gift I've found a set of old, silver sake cups that are badly tarnished, and in need of shining. When my mother used to polish the silver, I'd help her scoop the pink, caked cream out of the glass jar, and rub it between the tines of the forks and inside the round bowls of the spoons. Then we'd soak them, and run them under warm water before wiping the silverware off with a damp rag to make them shine. Unlike other household tasks, my mother could really lose herself in polishing the silver. Sometimes, she'd even hold out a piece in front of her to admire it. The black layer on the sake cups rubs off easily, and when I'm finished they're perfectly shiny.

≈

"Maybe it was sudden death syndrome," is what my doctor says at my yearly fall checkup, when I tell her the story of how my mother died. She tells me that it's actually possible for a person's heart to stop beating as a result of sudden fear. Maybe she saw a scary-looking fish, panicked, and died. It seemed extreme, but I could imagine it.

This "sudden death" does fit with my mother. In a way, she'd even prepared us for it over the course of life. Enduring and competent as she may have wanted to be, she wasn't always that dependable. When it was her turn to drive the Hebrew school carpool, usually we were the last ones to be picked up and the janitor had to wait around to turn off the lights and lock up. "Where's your mother?" the other kids in the carpool would ask. "It's getting dark. It's time for supper."

Once, my mother and I were walking on the hot cement squares that led to the beach. We were wearing the matching pink and orange flowered terrycloth beach robes that she'd made especially for us. I wasn't watching where I was going, and I stepped right on a hornet that stung me. I lunged onto my mother, screaming and wrapping my arms around her. But she abruptly pushed me off, probably shocked that I had jumped right onto her. Even after a few seconds, she didn't hug me or do anything to relieve my fright. But another time that same summer, she stood up for me. Her best friend, Honey, who always yelled at us in a way that I didn't think was fair because she wasn't our mother, reprimanded me for not eating the disgusting scrambled eggs she'd made for my lunch. "That's because you made it with margarine," my mother explained to her. "Anne only likes eggs cooked in butter." I couldn't believe it, but my mother was really on my side that time. You could never be completely sure of when she would come through.

Sometimes I'd complain to other mothers, my friends' mothers whom I trusted, about how mean my mother could be. But it was hard to get them to understand. When they'd see me come over with the little sweater that my mother had made for my Midge doll, they thought my mother must be perfect. Those were the days when everyone had two or three Barbies and a Ken doll, and later there was Skipper, "Barbie's little sister." After I begged and begged, my mother said, alright, I could have *one* doll. With just one, I figured I'd better be different, so I chose a red-haired Midge, "Barbie's best friend." When it was time to buy the clothes, my mother said, "Only one outfit." So I picked out the pretty garden dress that came with two plastic glasses of lemonade and two tiny straws. When I begged some more for the opera singer's dress, my mother refused, but instead she knit Midge a tiny, green sweater from the leftover yarn of an afghan she'd recently made. My friends' mothers thought it was amazing that my mother had actually knit my doll a sweater. It was almost impossible to prove that there was a problem with her. She was deceptively present in the world, even though she could be almost invisible as my mother.

When it came to Thanksgiving, my mother conveyed a sense of pride about our family, and I believed in it, too. It was very symmetrical. There were four siblings. My mother and Cecile were the two older girls, and Joe and Nate the two younger boys. They all grew up and got married, and each family had three children. We'd rotate the location of Thanksgiving every year—Boston for our family, New York for Cecile and Washington, where Joe and Nate lived.

There were no old people because the grandparents had died—their mother in her early forties of cancer and their father a few years after that. The four of them were all young when that happened. My mother, the oldest, was just twenty-five. And Nate was only thirteen. But no one ever used the word "orphan" to describe Nate. That was reserved for characters in books like *Oliver Twist* or *Nobody's Girl*, which was my favorite. Even though it was sad, it hadn't been too difficult, because they'd all helped each other. That was the story I'd been told and believed. Nate moved in with Cecile and Stu, who were already married by then and living in Queens. He became an older brother and an uncle at the same time to my cousins David, Jon and Miriam. And I envied them for getting to live with Nate. Joe finished college and went on to law school, which was conveniently located near Boston so that he could easily visit us on the weekends in Marblehead. The way I saw the picture, it was even romantic.

The core of Thanksgiving was just the four families. We never seemed to notice the lack of grandparents whom we had never known. When Thanksgiving was in Queens, sometimes Uncle Stu and Nate would drive off for an hour or so, in Stu's blue Rambler, and they'd return with some old people. Usually it would be my great-grandmother, and an old obscure cousin named Gussie Golding. And occasionally Great-Uncle Harry and Great-Aunt Martha would make a short visit, too. Great-Grandma would sit on the couch, her face very old and shriveled and wearing her turban-style hat, silently observing this young branch of the family whom she rarely saw. She looked especially small and shrunken sitting next to the equally stationary Gussie Golding, who was very large and always wore a colorful print dress. We'd topple around on the floor and play with the toys Gussie Golding brought us from the Ideal Toy Company, where she worked as a receptionist. Even though we didn't really talk to these people, I could feel their importance as relics of a past world that was somehow related to me, but that I had little to do with. Then they'd leave, and I'd forget about them until they'd make their appearance again a few years later. Our yearly family celebration of Thanksgiving was neatly packaged without the complications (or the texture) of older generations that inherently brought with them death, sadness, and evocation of a different layer of life.

This is the year for Boston. My father said he wanted to cook Thanksgiving dinner because it was our family's turn. But that obviously wasn't going to work, so we're gathering at the house of my cousin Annie, who lives in a remote suburb I hadn't heard of until now. We follow the complicated directions through a maze of intersecting streets and culs-de-sac, until we finally find the right house. There's a circular driveway in front that strangely reminds me of Joe and Helene's house in Bethesda, where Annie grew up.

There are fewer people than usual. Normally all the cousins come from up and down the east coast, and some from Spokane, Portland, and San Diego. But this year there are less of us. Of course my mother isn't here, and Ted is celebrating with his in-laws because it's an alternate year. Also there have been some divorces.

My father arrives with the turkey. "Do you think it will matter that I left this inside while it was cooking?" he asks, showing me the plastic package holding the gizzard and neck. I assure him it's okay, and suggest that he should just throw away the wrapped innards before anyone notices. Different relatives quietly ask how my father is faring. I report that between working three days a week at his consulting job, dinner with friends, and playing tennis, he's keeping busy. And he's just planned a ski trip over Christmas with some neighbors who have a place out West. Thanksgiving has changed for the better, less obligatory than it used to be. The year before Danny died was almost impossible to bear, with all of the tension and the desire to make things seem normal like always. Still, everyone had gathered that year for the ritual family picture, all twenty family members present, five in each family, all the kids a little taller than the last picture the year before, all the parents smiling. The next year, when Thanksgiving was only a month after Danny's death, I didn't think I'd survive it.

As I look around my cousin's unfamiliar living room, there's a lot of variety. Divorced and dead spouses have been replaced by new ones, who are now becoming part of the family fabric. And the youngest generation of my cousins' children, some of whom I've never seen before, compensates for the loss in numbers. This year one cousin has brought a friend, and he takes the family photo so that everyone can be in it and we don't have to do it by setting the timer.

We drive back to New York early Saturday morning, so we can be home for the rest of the weekend. On Sunday morning I make pancakes with the remaining frozen blueberries still left from Maine. Roy makes one last really big pancake, filling the whole frying pan with the batter, and the kids love that. We sit around the table while they lick the blueberry juice and syrup from their plates.

"Where's the Titanic?" Eli asks.

"At the bottom of the ocean," Roy answers him. "It sank a long time ago."

"How did it sink?" asks Eli.

"It got hit by an iceberg, a very big piece of ice," I say.

"Where in the ocean is it?" Eli's clearly pursuing a particular line of thought.

"I think it's near the North Pole," I answer, not knowing at all what I'm talking about. "Remember it was hit by a big piece of ice."

"Actually, that's not where it is," says Roy.

"Where's the captain?" asks Eli.

"He's buried. He died a very long time ago," Roy explains.

"Is he a skeleton?" Eli wants to know.

"Yes."

"Is Grandma Lois a skeleton?"

I don't answer, partly because I don't want to think about it, partly because I don't think she's a skeleton yet.

"Yes, she is," says Roy.

"Can we dig her up to see her skeleton?" Eli asks.

"No, we can't," says Roy. "It's much too deep."

"I could do it." Eli's voice is growing with excitement. "I'm a very good digger. Remember at the beach I dug so deep I got to the water."

"No, it's very, very deep," says Roy.

"I could do it with a machine."

"No," Roy says firmly. "It's too deep."

Seven

My father says he won't light the Chanukah candles at home by himself, so he's sent the old menorah to me. "The tall candle is called the *shamas*," I explain to Eli and Eva. "We use it to light the first candle on the first night. Tomorrow night we'll light two candles." When my mother had offered to give us a menorah as a Chanukah gift the first year of our marriage, I'd rejected it. "It would be a waste," I told her. "We'd never use it." I'd felt a little heartless, but at the time it still seemed necessary to let her know where I stood. I try to remember the blessings that we sang every year, my mother always off key, the rest of us dutifully joining in. Roy, normally an opponent of all religious ritual, sings a Yiddish rendition of "Oy, Chanukah," and the kids are on the floor laughing because Roy's song sounds like gibberish. I give the kids their presents and try to be happy about the candle lighting and singing.

My arguments with Roy haven't been too serious lately, but it's a delicate balance. As the winter starts to set in, I can tell he's getting a little sick of my quest for whatever it is I'm trying to figure out about my mother and me. "It would be easier if you could just have dinner ready a half hour earlier," he says. "That way the kids could get to sleep earlier, and so could we." Just because my office is at home now, he thinks that my work and getting dinner ready are the same. "You do it!" I snap back. "You be the one to get dinner ready, even just two nights a week. Or at least do the shopping on the weekends once in a while." I wonder whether a bad cold or flu is about to put one of us over the edge of our slightly teetering existence. Soon the kids will be on Christmas break and I'll have to figure out some activities for them.

The fact is that we're completely sleep deprived. Eva is now waking up three times a night. And she'll no longer be cooperative and just drink the juice I've left by her bed and go back to sleep. I check in with my friend, the child psychologist, who suggests that Eva's waking up so much in the night might have something to do with her processing my mother's death. He says I should show Eva some old photos of me and my mother and father, and of me and my grandmother. Maybe the pictures will reassure her of my presence next to my mother's absence. I ask my father to send me some old photo albums, and I find some snapshots that look just right for my purposes. Eva seems a little interested.

"When will it be my birthday?" she asks as I put her to sleep.

"In August, in the summer," I say.

"Who will hold the cake?" Eva asks.

"I will. I'll make you a cake and hold it, and you'll blow out the candles."

"Can Grandma Lois hold the cake?"

"No, I don't think she can."

"Can Papa Joel?"

"If you want him to, yes."

"Who are my grandmas?" she ventures on.

"Grandma Lois was your grandma. And Gloria is your grandma."

"Can Gloria be your mom?"

"No, Grandma Lois was my mom, and she always will be."

"Can you have a new Grandma Lois—a big one or a little one?"

"I don't think so."

"Grandma Lois died," Eva says. "She's *dead*."

"Yes, she is," I try to respond evenly.

"I love you, Mommy."

"I love you, too. Very, very much."

"Can you have a new Grandma Lois?" she wants to know again. But she doesn't wait for an answer. "I love you, Mommy," she repeats and nods off to sleep.

On New Year's Eve, Roy and I go out to a movie and have dinner at the bar of a fancy restaurant. Everyone else is wearing beads and sequined dresses, and dining on their $200-a-person dinners. We drink our champagne and watch the dressed-up revelers in their party hats as midnight strikes. In what seems like an absurd tradition, they shake their noisemakers like they really mean it. I can now officially say that my mother died last year, something I would never have forecasted last New Year's Eve. In only two more months an entire year will have passed and it hardly seems like she's dead at all.

≈

I sit shivering in my paper gown, on the edge of the examining table, waiting to see the doctor. If my mother hadn't been diagnosed with breast cancer when she was sixty-seven, just a year before she died, I wouldn't now be considered a "high risk" patient who needs to see a breast specialist. It didn't matter that she'd died of something else entirely. When my mother found the lump in her breast, the gynecologist said it was my responsibility to get checked regularly. I didn't like the doctor he sent me to first, so this year I'm trying someone new.

The first thing I notice is that she's wearing a head covering. Who would have ever expected that my doctor would turn out to be an Orthodox Jew? I tell her about my earlier mammograms, and how dutiful I've been about getting them every year since I turned thirty-five. I explain that when my mother was diagnosed with breast cancer she had been treated easily and successfully, and that her prognosis had been good, somehow believing that my mother's model recovery and my good behavior would have a positive effect on my status. I also tell her that my mother died of some type of sudden death syndrome, or at least that's what we think it might have been, hoping against hope that this piece of information would supersede her brief bout with breast cancer and clear me, too. I try to deliver all of this in a matter-of-fact way, but I hear my voice cracking and my eyes fill with tears. The doctor is steady and kind, and she tells me that I still need to be treated as "high risk," given my family history. I should continue to get annual mammograms, and to be checked by her yearly, too. She doesn't seem particularly daunted by any of this. She's calm and medical at the same time, and she seems good at her job. I decide I like her and sign up for another appointment next year.

It was nearly a year ago that I saw my mother for the last time, on that last visit when she and my father came to take care of Eli and Eva as an anniversary gift. It had been even more of a gift than I had known, not just the time alone with Roy— the afternoon at the Met, the leisurely drinks and dinner, the night to ourselves at the Soho Grand with the plush white towels and robes. When we returned home the next morning of that January weekend, after we caught up on their time with the kids, I embraced my mother in our living room on Riverside Drive. That was the most long-lasting part of what she'd given me, a true reunion after our time apart. It might have been the start of a new chapter between us, at the same time that it was an unknown goodbye.

As the anniversary of my mother's death approaches, I feel like I'm somehow running out of time, trying to figure out how much I loved my mother. In many ways I don't feel very different than I did a year ago. I worry that the kids sense my neediness.

"Who do you love more?" Eli asks me. "Me or yourself?" How do I answer this?

"That's a good question," I say. "I love us both very much." And then I think to add, "One reason I love myself so much is because I love you so much." Eli seems to like this and I'm pleased to have come up with it.

Eva's sleep patterns deteriorate further. She now wakes up four and even five times a night, and sometimes she won't even go to bed at bedtime. "I want you to stay with me forever, Mommy," she says. "I don't ever want to go to sleep." She keeps on asking me about Grandma Lois, and about whose mother is whose. "We all need sleep," I tell her in a rational voice. "We need sleep so we'll be happy, not angry and cranky in the morning." "I don't want to sleep," she keeps saying.

Yesterday in a calm moment I finally found some good dates for us to go to Club Med, and I booked the tickets. In a few weeks we'll all at last be sitting on a beach in the Bahamas. The thought melts some of my exhaustion. Maybe by then Eva will sleep again.

Literally overnight, Eva *does* sleep. She wakes up one morning and plainly states, "Mommy, I need to pee in the toilet." And that's it. In an instant, she's fully toilet-trained, and she's ready to go back to her more acceptable sleeping habits of a month before. This ordeal that has taken on dark thoughts of the true meaning of death, is no more and no less than a great developmental stride in the life of a two-year-old. The big propellers of life have won out again.

~

It was the end of the cold winter after Danny died when I first discovered the delight of swimming in a warm climate while the temperatures at home were freezing. As some sort of unusual compensation for Danny's death, my eccentric great-aunt Sylvia gave Ted a thousand dollars. Ted, ignoring her blatant favoritism, generously split the sum with me. And with my newfound money, I promptly booked a bargain charter flight to Jamaica.

I was probably at my most alienated over Danny when the money from Aunt Sylvia arrived. That same week I'd run into my old boss from the auction house on the street in Greenwich Village. As always he was gangly and awkward, but also a naturally cheerful man and he greeted me with a big hello. "How are you?" he'd asked innocently. In my harsh state, I didn't care at all about keeping up appearances and I answered him honestly, "Not so well, actually. My brother killed himself a few months ago." I watched him with a mixture of embarrassment and satisfaction as his mouth gaped open. He turned around 180 degrees and quickly walked in the other direction, and I never saw him again. My brother's death had effectively become part of my identity.

I had planned to make the trip to Jamaica alone, but at the last minute, a not-very-close friend from college, a woman named Bev who had a week to spare, heard I was going, and came along. There was a huge snowstorm, so Bev and I had to spend the first night of our trip at JFK. After a day and a night in the airport with Bev, I was intolerant of what I considered to be her entitled and protected ways, her obliviousness to the hardship I had painfully endured in my life.

Ragged and sleep deprived, and our six-day vacation now down to five days, we finally arrived in Montego Bay. We rented a car to drive to Negril, where we managed to find a little hotel, a place with thatched roof huts right on the edge of the cliffs overlooking the water.

Aside from eating jerk chicken, getting my hair braided, and keeping myself coated in sunscreen under the strong Caribbean sun, what I remember most about the trip was swimming for hours in the unbelievably warm, clear, pale turquoise water. I remember the great sense of relief I felt in that water.

Actually, I can also remember shrieking when I almost hit a boy on a bicycle when he rode out onto the dirt road, seemingly from nowhere. And there was also that one night when Bev and I sat at a bar drinking pretty pink rum drinks, the sound of the waves rolling in the background. Handsome Jamaican men would surround us, as seemed usual in Negril, and one especially charming man lavished his attention on me. As the night went on, Bev astutely seduced him in a way I could never have done, and they went off together. I went back to my little hut alone and angry, although also a little peaceful about being by myself, the wind blowing through the thin walls and thatched roof.

The next morning I put on my bathing suit and went down to the water. I swam for what must have been hours. These were not the chilly, dark, tingly waters of my childhood, but lovely, soothing, pale turquoise waters. I discovered I had great endurance, swimming back and forth along the entire length of the beach. Periodically, I'd stop and go to find my towel in the sand and dry off for a while. And then I'd return to the water again. The water washed over my anger at Bev. It softened the pain and sadness over the loss of Danny, and even quelled some of my rage at my mother, who was so unrightfully angry at me for being so sad. "Get some medication! Find someone to help you, if you're so unhappy!" her words echoed. And I let the water dissolve them.

After that trip to Jamaica, I came back to New York ready to start things fresh. It was almost spring, and it seemed the right time to thoroughly clean out every corner and crack of my new apartment. I had just moved into a small, bright, one-bedroom place at the end of MacDougal Street that my father had helped me buy. It was a great deal, and the old woman who'd lived there until she died had left an old trundle bed couch, which I remade with futons and covered with deep blue flowered Asian fabric. She'd also left an old iron bed, which looked really nice once I spray-painted it black and got a new mattress and box spring. I'd chosen a different very pale pastel color to paint each of the three rooms.

I wiped out the apartment with even more vengeance than my mother would have done, determined to make it immaculate. The one remaining sore spot in the apartment was the bathtub, which was badly worn and stained. I used a special product for cleaning stained porcelain, a powder called "Zud" that was like Ajax but a lot stronger. When the Zud didn't completely work, I tried adding bleach. And then the fumes started to get strong. I was kneeling inside the tub, scouring it with rags drenched in cleaning concoction, when I started to get dizzy and felt like I was about to faint.

Worried that I'd gotten carried away with the ferocity of my cleaning, possibly at my own expense, I got out of the tub and went into my bedroom to lie down. I knew enough to think of the psychological implications of what I was doing, and I called Ted to let him know that maybe I'd been risking my own safety. "I think I may have breathed in too many chemicals," I told him. "I'm scared I went too far." But Ted didn't seem to understand what I was getting at. When I said I was worried that maybe I was identifying *too* much with Danny, he responded, "I envy your pain," and then changed the subject to something else. I hung up, and swallowed down four large glasses of water, hoping I could sleep off any damage I might have done.

≈

It's almost the end of winter, and remarkably we've made it to the Bahamas. Here we are, Roy, Eli, Eva, and me, in Eleuthera. The sand is truly pink, and the gentle lapping waves are the palest of turquoise. As I gaze out at the sea, at what I imagine to be a distant continent, the almost imperceptible tingle of my mother is all around me. It's as if she's taken on some kind of ethereal form, as pleasant as the light breeze. I'm certain, even if it's as fleeting as these moments, that I've touched on a piece of her essence, a piece I'd never been able to touch in her lifetime. Maybe this is the sensation I've been waiting for all of these months. It's a delectable few days of vacation when Roy and I sit by the water's edge and read books, the water quietly lapping up at our feet, Eli and Eva engaged in their own activities in the kids camps. When camp hours are over, they come to play in the water, too, and dig in the fine sand and build castles. We're all peacefully together, happy in the perfectly temperate air.

When we return to New York, we've reached the beginning of March, and my mother has now been dead for one full year. While the months and days amount to the right amount of time, nothing obvious happens. I'm still left with a blurry idea of what it means that my mother is dead. Ted says that he's now experienced all the seasons since my mother's death, I think meaning that he's now come through an essential journey of acceptance. I know the year has made a difference, but it doesn't have the real power to divide. I'm still left with a picture of my mother's death that's not at all in focus.

Eli and I pass a dead pigeon on the sidewalk. "I hate seeing dead birds," he says. "I hate seeing all dead animals. It makes me too sad."

"It makes me sad, too." I say.

"Will the bird ever live again?" Eli asks me.

"No," I answer.

Later in the afternoon the four of us are out walking. "I saw a dead bird this morning," Eli tells Roy. "It makes me very sad to see a dead bird because it won't live anymore."

"Yes, it's very sad," says Roy.

"It's dead just like Grandma Lois is dead. We'll never see her face again," he says.

Eight

My mother said that "unveilings" weren't part of official Jewish tradition. People chose to have ceremonies for unveiling tombstones more as a matter of comfort. There was no Jewish law about it. But it's now more than a year after my mother has died and my father wants an unveiling. I've never been to one before, but from what I can tell it won't have the pain or the chaos of the funeral, so I go up to Andover by myself and leave Roy with the kids.

By chance the manuscript I've taken with me to read on the plane is about the state of ecstasy. I fixate on a passage that says it is possible for a very anxious person who is unaccustomed to experiencing real happiness to be so overwhelmed when they encounter it, that they can *die*. It says that statistically an inordinate number of Japanese businessmen die of heart attacks while vacationing—where else but in the Great Barrier Reef! They leave the tension of their everyday lives, and without this structure, in a relaxed state they actually expire. Maybe this is my answer. Maybe my mother's death was a matter of her being taken off guard by being happy. Maybe it wasn't fear or anxiety, but happiness that took her life away. If she had that much happiness in her, in the beauty of the faraway Australian water, then maybe I could be happy, too.

It turns out that my mother knew her Jewish traditions well. My father, Ted, Janet, and I watch as the gravestone is unveiled by the rabbi. It's not especially emotional. The rabbi says a few prayers, officially joining my mother's grave with the others in the cemetery. On the way out, we pass the other plots. The rabbi gossips with us about some of the other, more colorful recent deaths of the congregants, one even involving adultery and murder. My mother's death, it occurs to me, has a story attached to it, too, one that can now be added to the others.

I'm starting to see my mother from the outside. Maybe that's what unveilings are for, to veer away from the ongoing rending of emotions, to situate the death as part of life. My mother had never done that with death. For my mother, who had absorbed so much fatality, death itself had remained an open, unresolved chapter that just kept on resurfacing and causing more injuries along the way. Maybe this was something I could do for her now, or more significantly something I could do for the future of my family, to make the deaths part of the material of life.

～

I can tell by the way Roy answers that it's his mother. At first, I figure she must be calling to wish me a happy birthday, although she's usually the first birthday call of the day, and now that I think of it, it's strange that she'd be a day late. But Roy's eyes are watery when he hangs up the phone. "It's bad," he says. "Gloria has cancer." We walk toward the bedroom, so the kids won't hear. "It's already spread from her colon to her lungs." He starts to cry, and I put my arm around him, but he pushes me away. He's too shocked for consolation.

"How long does she have? Did she say?" I ask.

"Maybe less than a year," Roy answers.

It's only been a few months more than a year since my mother died, and we now have Gloria's death in front of us. But this death will be different, because we know about it ahead of time. Even though the specter of Gloria's cancer isn't always overt, we now live with another layer of anticipation.

Roy won't be spending much time with me and the kids on Deer Isle this year, because Gloria's chemo treatments are scheduled to begin in August. He wants to be near home. And also his job at the university is getting tense, so he's more uneasy than usual about being away.

It's a break to get to Deer Isle again, to get away from our New York trappings. Even though Roy's not around much and even though the regular babysitter decides to leave early for college and I'm mostly on my own to balance Eli and Eva, and camp and swimming, and the residual office details, still it's a break to get to Deer Isle again. I feel remarkably grounded this August, like I know the turf.

"Old MacDonald had a farm . . ." Eva sings every verse of the song, imitating every animal sound with relish. She has just turned three and whenever we get into the car, she taunts Eli with her singing from the moment I buckle her into her car seat. "Stop!" screams Eli, who is driven to tears by Eva's singing. I can't tell if it's intentional, but she succeeds in sparking Eli off, and the effect is maddening.

The one thing they unite on is pooping and peeing, which they seem to do constantly. "I have to go to the bathroom!" one or the other calls out from the back seat just after we've driven about a mile. "Me, too!" the other chimes in. I've taken to traveling with a roll of toilet paper wherever we go. I get to know every public outhouse and supermarket bathroom in the vicinity. When we are outside, together they scamper around to pick out a rock to pee on at the beach, or a bush to kneel behind.

Roy comes for a short one-week visit, and he brings the distress of New York and of Gloria with him. Our different approaches to dealing with death and illness grate against each other.

"Did Leon ask the doctor what the side effects of Gloria's chemo will be?" I ask. "And what happens if this course of treatment doesn't work?"

"Leon's waiting for the doctor to tell *him*." Roy's tone is slightly aggravated.

"But don't they want to know what to expect? Or if there are other options?"

Roy's family doesn't ask a lot of questions. They accept that the doctor will know best. It's a mindset that's hard for me to accept; I want to shake them into action. But this is Roy's upbringing, and he understands the temperament.

Other than Roy, his whole family now lives in New Jersey. It's as if they've just drifted to the location, not like they really belong there. For all of Roy's childhood they'd lived in Long Island. Growing up they'd visited their cousins who lived on the Jersey shore. And a couple of times they'd rented a house there for a week or two in the summer. But other than that it wasn't clear why they decided to pick up and move there. When Leon retired from the insurance business and they moved to the Jersey shore, Gloria and Leon left their tight circle of life-long friends in Long Island, to live in a town an hour and a half away. Later Roy's brothers followed them. His younger brother left his Manhattan apartment and moved to a town right next to his parents. And eventually his older brother moved back from California with his family and bought a home in another New Jersey suburb. When Roy and I first met and I asked him about his parents, he told me they lived "somewhere in New Jersey," but couldn't remember the name of the town. That had impressed me, that he could be detached like that, but still care about them.

Gloria and Leon don't even like the beach. When we visited them in New Jersey, on days when it was warm, they could sometimes be convinced to take a walk on the boardwalk. But if I suggested that we walk in the sand by the water, or maybe take a towel in case we wanted to swim, they'd grimace. "The sand is dirty," Leon would say. "And uncomfortable," Gloria would agree. And mostly we'd just stay inside with the too-cold air conditioning on, or sometimes take a stroll in the neighborhood and pass the time talking about which houses were for sale.

I wonder what they really think of me, of my family who yelled at each other at the dinner table, of my brother who committed suicide, of my father who changed jobs every few years when he could no longer see eye to eye with his bosses and then dragged the whole family along with him from state to state. And what they really thought of my mother who was so tied to her Hebrew school. If there's one thing Roy's family has a strong opinion about, it's organized religion. They're adamantly opposed to it, the whole family. They celebrate Passover on the closest Saturday to the date, to make it more convenient. On Rosh Hashanah, Gloria once said to me, "Why aren't people going to work today anyway?" acting like she didn't know. I'm pretty sure she did know and was trying to make a statement, but it was hard to read exactly what she meant. Roy's family can be needling that way, not always direct.

Outwardly there's a link between Roy's parents and mine, and they all seemed to appreciate that. They all grew up in New York City. Gloria, Leon, and my father all went to City College at around the same time. Leon and my father even discovered a mutual acquaintance from their days at Bronx Science and Townsend Harris high schools. But really the sensibilities of the families are far apart.

At Roy's family gatherings, the television is always on, the predominantly male household absorbed in football or baseball or whatever sport is in season, a far cry from my mostly nonathletic family. Around the table, there's a lot of sarcastic joke telling that makes me feel quiet. Sometimes they misread something I've said, and laugh like I'd meant it to be comical or cynical, even though that's not my intent at all.

When Roy first introduced me to his family, he thought Gloria and I would unite in our common interest in books. Gloria used to work in a bookstore, and a lot of times she'll recommend a novel she's just finished, or ask me about a new book she's heard of and whether it's causing a stir in the publishing business. But even reading is something we seem to do differently. Gloria can easily read two or three books a week, happy to escape into a different world. I, despite my profession, read slowly, less willing to allow myself to be transported to a fictional place, more likely to be driven by the emotion of the writing. Gloria could never be the replacement for the missing parts of my own mother. As much as I declared my dissimilarities with the mother who gave birth to me, she recognized when I was really sad or upset, even if she was the cause of it. And I could always get her to go for a walk with me on the beach. I might prefer her to be different, but I could not replace her.

I met Roy eight years ago when we were set up on a blind date arranged by Roy's cousin and a mutual friend. I was skeptical, but figured it would at least be a half-hearted attempt to get away from my sort-of boyfriend, who was seeing someone else at the same time and who was never going to add up to a meaningful relationship. When I first heard Roy's Long Island accent (which he still denies having) on the phone, my doubts continued. Besides that, he was Jewish and a lawyer, which would be much too high on the list of my mother's approved criteria.

"I'm not saying he'll be the father of your children," my friend who set us up said. "Just have dinner. I'm sure you'll like each other enough for that." The dinner happened, and Roy was kind, and confident. "May I?" he asked without question, as he took the bill to pay it. There was not a hint of the second-guessing that I'd experienced on countless other first dates.

Maybe I was at last ready to stop resisting what might be comfortable. Maybe my preconceived idea of romance that seemed to require drama and gloom was ready to be shed. When I considered it, I realized that Danny had been dead now for nearly ten years. Whomever I met from hereon in would never know Danny, and the passage of time would make it so that they wouldn't even really know him through me. Maybe I could take an unfamiliar step into the world that was in front of me. Roy was self-assured and thoughtful, and I was willing to find out more.

~

My father has begun talking more about Judith Taylor. Ted and I already knew that he was never at home on weekends when we tried to call him. But finally he's given us her phone number. "If you need to reach me and I'm not home," he says. "I might be at Judith's." That was a big breakthrough.

Sometimes he would mention that he and Judith had given a dinner party, or attended the bar mitzvah of Judith's cousin's son, or even gone to a concert at Tanglewood together. But if I asked whether Judith might want to join him and come up to Maine, or maybe come with him to New York on his next visit, he'd say, "No. It's not like that."

The biggest issue that my father seemed to have with Judith was that she didn't like to travel. "Not like your mother," he'd say. "Your mother was always game for adventure." It was true that my parents had traveled together—they had skied out West, and hiked in the Dolomites, and there had been trips to France, Italy, Greece, and Turkey, and of course, there had been three visits to Israel. And finally there was the trip to New Zealand and Australia. But my father was romanticizing. My mother was not adventurous, and I doubted she would have gone on most of those trips if he hadn't pushed her. What motivated my mother was that she belonged to what appeared to be a well-functioning family, and travel might have been part of that. So was skiing and tennis. My mother conceded that she'd nearly failed gym class in school, but after decades of practice, she'd become a reasonable tennis player and her serve went forcefully over the net, even if it still looked pretty spastic. Skiing was a particularly unlikely feat for my mother, but with sheer determination she succeeded. Intrepidly she graduated from the bunny slopes to the intermediate trails at that top of the mountain. And our traditional Christmas trip came to be skiing in Vermont.

After my mother died, my father continued his travels on his own. Last winter he went skiing in Vail with a neighbor. This year he's planning another trip to the Austrian Alps with an elderhostel group. Had it not been for the diagnosis of prostate cancer a few months ago, he'd right now be bicycling in Vermont.

The prostate cancer appeared almost exactly a year after my mother died, as if waiting for my father to be galvanized enough to manage it. He said he didn't need my help or Ted's. He could handle driving into Boston for the radiation treatments without us. "I'm fine," my father said. He'd already asked for a few days off from his consulting job. "It's an easy drive to Mass General and back. I can make it in thirty minutes each way, as long as I don't schedule the treatments for rush hour."

Real recovery, though, required time, and care. And that was when he started admitting Judith into his life. He moved into her house for a couple of weeks and let her tend to him. The relationship made sense. They came from the same Jewish community. Their spouses had died within the same month. And Judith even bore a slight physical resemblance to my mother, although she was gentler and kinder.

My father brings up his worries about the grandchildren. "I think it will confuse them," he says, "to meet Judith." More than that, I think he feels guilty that the grandchildren will forget their grandmother altogether, and he probably worries about forsaking Ted and me, too, by letting Judith in. To me, it always seemed that my parents' marriage lacked a sense of ease of companionship that I thought marriage was supposed to have. But still my father has a keen sense of duty about being married, to my mother that is.

"Eva and Eli would love to meet Judith," I encourage him. The fact is that Eva needed a photograph to even know who Grandma Lois was. And Eli hadn't mentioned her name in months. "They'll have plenty of room for Judith, and will still remember their grandmother," I say. It was during those weeks after the radiation when my father must have come to understand, maybe for the first time, that a companion like Judith could provide tenderness.

In November, Gloria usually makes a big lunch for all the family birthdays that come in the fall. But this year we have the celebration in our apartment instead. Roy plans the menu, choosing special dishes that he thinks his family will appreciate—macaroni and cheese, and roast pork. I gather recipes from my friend Katherine, who's a great chef—macaroni with three cheeses and red peppers, and a pork casserole baked with lentils in a special clay pot that I borrow from Katherine. Roy watches with annoyance as his family picks at the food I've taken so much time to prepare. "Of course they won't touch the salad," he whispers to me in the kitchen. "Pickles are the only green vegetable they've ever heard of." They do enjoy the chocolate birthday cake that I've covered with thick chocolate frosting and decorated with all their names. "This is really good," says Leon, "as good as store bought." He means this as a compliment. Roy tells me that I'm generous to have prepared this party for his family. But I don't feel generous in the least. I'm incensed as I put the two uneaten pans of macaroni and cheese in the freezer for some other time.

The year is long. We try to visit Gloria and Leon regularly, and it occurs to me that Gloria and I are getting used to each other. New Jersey may be an inexplicable place for them to live, but Gloria takes great pleasure in decorating the living room. She shows me her new purchases from the flea market—a new table, a flowerpot, a small stool with an embroidered cushion on top. She regularly rearranges the furniture, to keep things interesting and alive. And I find myself getting comfortable in their home. Hanging everywhere are tapestries and posters and Japanese prints, which she also regularly rotates. I imagine it must have been a lot like this in Roy's house growing up. And there are arrangements of dolls made out of yarn, the handiwork of Gloria's mother, Pauline, whose skill as a milliner is renowned in the family.

Eli and Eva don't seem to notice that anything is amiss. Gloria's responded much better than anticipated to the chemo treatments, and after several months, the doctor is now predicting he may still have more than a year of life ahead. And she hasn't lost her hair yet, although we're told that it will happen eventually. She still has the energy to have water fights with the kids with balloons and water pistols she's picked up at a garage sale. And she still sends Leon out to pick up Happy Meals at McDonald's, knowing it will provoke Roy and me and that the kids will love eating their French fries and slurping the milk shakes.

I notice that Gloria has softened. She's stopped saying things like, "I'm now a member of the Cancer Society" and making caustic jokes about death like she used to. When my mother died, she and Leon drove all the way to Andover for the funeral, and then turned around and left before the ceremony even happened. She never even witnessed the speeches or crowds or the reverence for my mother. They needed to make it home before dark, she'd later explained, as though this were something I could possibly understand amidst the chaos of my mother's death. In the past months, Gloria has become yielding toward me. She surprises me one day when she asks me to give her a haircut. I've always admired Gloria's thick, straight, pure white hair, bluntly cut in a straight line a little below her chin. With her hair and her large-framed glasses, she has her own distinct style. When I pick up the scissors I can see that her hair has become straggly, either because she hasn't had the strength to get it cut like she usually does, or maybe because of the effect of all the chemo and radiation. I try to trim the ends evenly, like they used to be.

Between Roy and me things are getting more brittle. The reality of my mother's death begins to merge more easily with life, while Gloria's looms ahead. I recognize Roy's fastidiousness mounting as things slip further out of his control. Even when it's hot, he refuses to open the windows more than a slot, saying that's enough and claiming it's better for the air circulation. He gets absurdly angry if I'm fifteen minutes late. He's neither interested nor appreciative when I report on the subway jams I've encountered on the way home from work, or about the time it takes to buy the groceries and get dinner on the table, or getting the kids' lunches packed for school in the morning. I want to fling the windows open and let the air blow in. When I'm driving in the car with just the kids, I blast Beatles music that they now love, and we all sing.

I know I have no right to be angry. He's worried about Gloria, and his job is really getting to him. The politics have become oppressive, even for Roy who's usually good at dealing with that type of thing. "Maybe it's time for a different job," I say when he tells me about the latest antics of the board members. But we both know that there's too much to wade through now to attempt any real change. The year drags along, without a clearing in sight.

Nine

"I'm into you today, Mommy," says Eva when she comes pattering into our bed this morning at dawn. We're back in our Deer Isle haven, unpacked for the month and happily settled into our round house. Moist, cool air fills the room. At nearly four, Eva's skin is plump and delicious. I touch her cheek, and can see that the swelling from the spider bite she got in her sleep the first night we arrived is going down. I can again detect the natural large almond shape of her eye as her face begins to lose its distortion.

I hug her, and we play under the sheets. It's a relief to leave the world of illness and death behind for a while. Cancer or no cancer, Roy will be here for three whole weeks this year. He's finally left his job, and the new one doesn't start until the last week of the month.

I'm glad, too, that Eva's face should be back to its normal shape by the time her new glasses arrive next week. Just at the last minute as I was getting everything organized to leave New York for the month, I brought Eva to her yearly medical checkup, just like usual. It was time for the eye chart, and no one was paying any particular attention until the doctor and I realized that Eva wasn't joking when she said she couldn't read the letters. The doctor tried holding up a picture of a monkey riding a bicycle, and Eva couldn't tell what that was either, even from only a few feet away.

We were lucky that the ophthalmologist had an appointment left that last week in July. That's when we found out that Eva, the child of two parents, each with perfect vision, turned out to be severely far-sighted, and one of her eyes was significantly out of sync with the other. "The weaker eye is already relying on the stronger eye to work," the doctor told me, as he wrote out Eva's eyeglass prescription. I was shocked at the diagnosis, and felt enormously guilty that I could have been so oblivious to it. "Should we pick up the glasses when we get back from Maine, in September?" I asked. "Actually, I'd go right over to Broadway and get them right now," said the doctor.

Trying my best to be as matter-of-fact as the doctor was, I explained to Eva that we were going to pick out a new pair of glasses. "But I don't want to wear glasses now," she said weakly, much too weakly for her usually forceful personality. Once in the store, Eva adjusted. "I want a pink pair and a purple pair," she said. We tried on twenty or thirty pairs and admiringly chose frames that were blue and green, to match her eyes I pointed out. I gave the store our address in Maine, and they said we'd have them at our doorstep in about a week. To care for the glasses, I should wash them in soapy water every night, and dry them with a paper towel, they told me.

Roy and I return from lunch at our favorite Deer Isle café, and Eva and the babysitter are sitting on the front steps waiting for us. "My glasses came, Mommy." Eva hands me the box. I untape the brown paper and then the bubble wrap, and there inside is the painted metal case with the dogs on it, the same one Eva had picked out in the store. When she puts them on, they look different than they did when we chose them. The lenses, which are real, magnify her eyes. This time she doesn't look like a little girl trying on glasses; she looks like a little girl who wears glasses.

On and off, she tests them. I watch her begin to see the world differently. We're driving around in the car when she leans toward me. "I didn't know you were wearing those earrings that are shaped like a leaf, Mommy. Your face is much closer now." To Roy she says, "Dad, your hair is brown." Later that afternoon when Roy leads her down the dirt path that we walk daily to the swimming pond, she tells him, "They put more pebbles on the path since yesterday."

"Can you see better now, Eva?" I ask her once we're back at the house and getting ready for dinner.

"No, everything just looks different," she says.

And then she runs to the bathroom and looks in the mirror, and I follow her. "I look funny," she says.

"You look beautiful," I tell her, my heart cracking a little as I witness this moment of change in my daughter's perception of herself. "When you go to sleep, I'll wash the glasses off for you and put them next to your bed, so you can put them on in the morning," I tell her. The truth is that I really don't know anything about wearing glasses, and I'm trying to sound like I do. Even though I'm her mother, Eva will always know more about this than I will.

It's easy to meld into a relaxed spirit this summer. But my father's visit disrupts our pace, especially because I'd been anticipating something better. When we visited him on our way up here, he'd seemed more comfortable. When we'd pulled into his driveway in what turned out to be the middle of the night and woke him from his sleep, he'd been unguarded and sweet. In the morning he played with Eli and Eva while I prowled around the house. I noticed that over the months my father had quietly cleared out almost all of my mother's possessions, although he'd left two flannel nightgowns and a few scarves in the corner of her dresser drawer, and there was still a belt of hers hanging in the closet. There was a distinct emptiness of my mother's presence that I hadn't felt before. And I supposed my father must have felt it, too, even though he didn't talk about it. As we continued the trip up to Maine, I'd missed my mother and felt tenderly toward my father.

But now he's awkward and yearning for attention, and I hate that I'm begrudging with him. We take him on the ferry to Isle au Haut and I point out the seals, but he keeps missing them when they jump out of the water. "Isn't it magnificent here?" I try to direct him toward all of the surrounding beauty of the granite islands set in the dark blue water. But it's as though he just can't see it. "It's too sunny out on the water," is his response. "And the wind could blow your hat away out here." In the playground he hits the tetherball too hard and it crashes into Eli's head.

I know a lot of the problem is my lack of tolerance. The kids both seem happy with my father's visit. Eli has taken to calling him "Pops." And Eva has come up with a new nickname, too. "Hey, Papa Joel-ie!" she yells. "Come see my new tie-dye shirt. It's drying on the porch." The shirt-making kit that my father brought as Eva's birthday gift is a big success. But I can't help it, when he drives off to Andover, I'm happy to continue the rest of our time on our own.

≈

We're all sad when we have to drop Roy off at the Bangor airport. When he comes back in a week, it will be time to pack up and drive home and no one's ready for that either. "Daddy, do you have to go?" Eva says. "When you come back will we still have time to swim some more in the pond?" asks Eli. Tears well up in my eyes as we wave goodbye. And Roy looks sad when he turns around one last time before walking onto the runway.

On the way back to Deer Isle, Eli and Eva bicker incessantly. They've already eaten all the snacks, and we've stopped for ice cream, and we're not even halfway there yet. I swerve over to the side of the road. "If you don't stop fighting right now, we're staying right here!" I threaten. They're a little surprised, and for a few minutes they stop. But then they're at it again, all the way back to Deer Isle.

Even once we get home, they're still arguing, and I'm starting to yell, too. In the bath, Eli throws water on Eva and she starts crying. "Give me a fucking break!" I scream, instantly realizing my vast indiscretion. But we're all laughing hysterically. "That was very, very wrong of me," I apologize as we all continue to laugh uncontrollably.

"What happened?" asks Eva, still too small to understand.

"Mom said the f-word," says Eli.

"What is it?" asks Eva.

"*I'm* not going to say it," says Eli as we all laugh and laugh, finding our balance again.

As our summer ends, it seems to have reached a perfect state. This last week is sunny and lovely, just as it's supposed to be. The swimming is beautiful. I'm blissful as I take my final strokes and emerge onto the banks of the pond. The late August sun is still warm. I find a sunny spot to spread out my towel, and nod at the familiar locals and vacationers who share the allure of this bucolic place. Once my bathing suit is almost dry, I round up Eva, who's playing with our local babysitter Emily. Eva has to be cajoled with a cookie to leave her sand pile, because it's time for me to drive Emily home. Eli stays behind with some New York neighbors, who have surprisingly turned up this week at our Lily Pond paradise. They say they'll look after Eli while I'm gone, and they've brought a canoe with them. Eli's excited about that.

When I return to the pond with Eva, all seems as usual. If there's anything impossible about the scene, it's only that it's so typically lovely. Eva, still sleeping after the car ride, lies easily down on the blanket. I wave to Eli, who's playing at the water's edge, and open my book, at the same time keeping an eye out for Eli. What I see are the comings and goings of the canoe, and children happily splashing in the water.

And then imperceptibly the mood changes. I begin to hear words in the air—words that are unaccountably echoing and repeating. "A man, about forty . . . last seen a couple of hours ago . . . entered the pond in a wet suit . . ." They're saying he has MS, but that he's a good swimmer. "His parents dropped him off at the pond. A couple of hours ago." No one really seems to know him, but that's not very surprising because almost all of the people at the pond today are out-of-towners. It's the end of August and all of the local kids have already gone back to school. The conversations begin to gain momentum. The man's parents have come back to find him, but they can't. They've lost track of him. I realize that I must have been dropping off Emily when the man everyone's talking about went out into the water. The New Yorkers with the canoe offer to take the man's parents out into the pond, to go look for him. They all get in, and someone shoves the canoe off from the beach.

Sitting on blankets and towels on the grass by the pond's edge, people are getting concerned. The canoe returns, but there's no new information. They decide to go out again in the canoe, but this time maybe they'll stop and get out, to search on the paths around the pond. Maybe the man had gone for a walk after his swim. That's when the buzzing turns into panic. I thought the missing man had MS. How could he go for a walk? What is everyone talking about? And why on earth do the people keep going out in a small canoe to look for this man?

"I think we should try to get some help," I finally say. Someone reaches in her bag for her cell phone, to dial 911, but all of us being out-of-towners, we don't know that 911 doesn't work in these reaches of Maine.

I get the kids out of the water and walk them up the path to the car, and by now the action has escalated. An official station wagon, the Deer Isle version of an ambulance, has arrived. People are gathered around, and now they're really talking. "Is there anything I can do to help?" I ask. "Maybe I could go home and call for a helicopter." Somehow I thought that helicopters were what you were supposed to use to find drowned bodies. But I'm told that it's better to use a boat to look for the man. And a boat is already on its way, a special boat with trenchers.

"What's going on?" the kids want to know.

"A man got lost," I say.

I leave it at that. And so far, they don't ask anything else, and I haven't said anything that's not true. For the past two and a half years, I've been consciously saving the details of my mother's death until the kids are older, so they won't be afraid of swimming. This summer Eli has made great strides. At camp he was awarded the "most energized bunny doggy paddle," and at six-and-a-half he's very proud of this. Eva has spent almost every day this August rolling around at the water's edge, splashing and swimming with her "floaties" attached to her still pudgy biceps. It's been a great summer for swimming.

The next day our friend Andrea arrives for a visit. After our hellos, she tells me that she's heard some bad news on the radio on her drive up.

"Rain?" I ask, my attention drawn instinctively toward planning our daily activities.

"A drowning at the Lily Pond in Deer Isle," she says. "A man with MS." That's how I find out for sure what I already knew. I tell Andrea that the Lily Pond is actually where we swim, and because it's a spectacularly beautiful day, and the kids want to go swimming, that's where we go. Despite the warmth of the day, there are no cars parked on the edge of the road at the head of the path that leads to the pond. We keep on going, and when we come into the clearing, there's the pond. It's completely calm, reflecting the world around it, with not a soul in sight. The kids jump into the water and I frolic around with them, but can't bring myself to take my usual swim. It's too spooky.

Later that day, I track down a friend who's a local and who seems to know everybody and everything on this small island, to find out what really happened in the pond. The man with MS was in his mid-forties, she tells me, and his illness had become unbearable to him. And he had become completely dependent on his parents, which made it even worse. "Each day brought him terrible pain," she says. "Only a few years before, he was a shining star. He was going to get married, until the disease took over." We'd seen him just last Sunday when he'd come down to the Lily Pond. Didn't I remember? We'd all been at the pond together that afternoon, when he came there in his walker with his parents to survey the idyllic scene. I sort of did remember. "He asked his parents to bring him to that same spot yesterday afternoon, and then to go do some errands or something, while he took a swim." That's when he went out into the pond and never came back.

Now there's a reason for the drowning, a human story. The man with MS must have been tremendously miserable, in pain and frustration and without an option. But did the scene for his death have to be in a public beautiful place like the Lily Pond? And what about the way he'd treated his parents? It seemed like such a cruel setup, but then again, I tell myself, that's part of what being in pain can be about.

I worry vaguely about how my mother's drowning is surfacing again, how it haunts me and how I might unwittingly be transmitting that to my children. But as I try to envision the man drowning in the Lily Pond, I'm aware that really the thing that disturbs me about this death isn't my mother. It's Danny. It's the man's similarity to Danny, who also chose to end his own life, that has now ruined the peace of the Lily Pond, the place of refuge that over the years I had learned to inhabit and trust. Maybe I had been right all along to know that deep down it wasn't safe.

Danny had planned his death, too. Although Danny was different. Physically he had been vital. The pain he could no longer bear was his own mental anguish. And Danny's death had been horribly violent. There were no beautiful ponds, no peaceful settings with birds and rocks and trees all around.

Nearly two decades have now passed since Danny's died, and still when I hear a siren I think of the screeching ambulance that must have carried his bloody, messy body from the restaurant where he worked in Providence to the city hospital. He had cut up his body with a kitchen knife, right into the intestines, right before the eyes of his boss at the restaurant, a woman who must never have been able to fathom what happened in front of her.

There had been bad signs. His alarming phone calls, filled with rage about his monstrous boss, had frightened me and Ted. Neither of us could understand the degree of his hatred for that woman. Only later did we come to recognize that through no fault of her own she probably stood for my mother. A couple of weeks before he killed himself, when Danny was visiting in Andover, he was alone with my mother, and he'd torn off the T-shirt he was wearing and slashed it up, right in front of her. My mother had been terrified, but she didn't say a word about it to anyone. Except for when she told us about it after Danny died, and then she never mentioned it again.

Danny was scared about what he was about to do. Two nights before the night of his death, he called my father saying he'd sliced his finger and he was worried about the cut. My

father could hear his fear, but he couldn't possibly compre-
hend the real meaning behind his words. And then Danny
went through with his ghastly plan. The doctors thought he
must have been on drugs to endure the pain he'd inflicted on
himself. But the autopsy proved that his blood was clean. His
intentions had been pure.

For years I could feel the violence he committed to his
body quietly etched on my own. I had been his champion, his
companion. We were allies, especially in our shared disdain
for our mother. "You must be so angry at him," people would
repeat to me endlessly after Danny died. But I didn't know
what they meant. I loved him deeply, and missed him beyond
belief. And for years I pledged to myself that I'd keep on being
the living part of him in this world. Even though ultimately
we were different. He was dead and I was alive.

The conflicted grief I have for my mother, I now see, has been
bound up in the ongoing pain I still carry for Danny. By wind-
ing the pain of Danny's death with my mother—with her life
and her death—I was passing along the very legacy I wanted more than anything to be free of. The echo of suicide and
death that was part of my mother's way of being did not have
to be mine. If I could just distinguish that invisible piece of
my mother that still lived inside me, maybe I could be free to
accept her. And maybe with that, I could at last admit the real
loss of Danny.

It's Danny, not my mother, and certainly not the man who
drowned in the Lily Pond, who has ruined my sense of sanctuary. I force myself to swim out far into the pond one more time
before we return to New York for the fall.

Ten

The air is dirty and noisy. Eli observes how big the buildings are, and how many people there are, and how many traffic lights. Every year when we return from Maine, we say the same thing. Maybe we should be living in a place where the breezes are fresh, the pace is slower, and where we can spend more time hanging around with our children. But this year it seems like we might really mean it. "Maybe upstate," Roy says. "We could commute from somewhere near Rhinebeck, and you could have an office at home. Let's make a trip up there to look at some houses."

"I'd prefer a life that has nothing to do with the city," I say. "No commuting, a place near the beach."

On our way back from dinner, Roy and I see a man get hit by a car. He flies up into the air and then his body thuds to the ground and he lies unconscious on the street. Repelled, and gravitated to the scene at the same time, I wonder if we should call someone. But the sirens are already screeching, the man's body surrounded by ambulances and curious passersby. The precariousness of our lives is tangible. "Let's leave," I say.

On our first visit to Gloria and Leon in September, we witness the damage of the past month—the full accumulation of the chemo treatments. Gloria has been transformed into an old, gaunt person, "a cancer patient," as she says.

"We really have to visit regularly now," Roy says.

"I know," I agree. "The kids need to remember their grandmother while they can still play with her."

"We may not have much time left," Roy dares to say. But Eli and Eva only see what's in front of them. They don't seem to notice that Gloria has changed, even though she now wears a scarf on her head.

Sitting in Gloria and Leon's living room, my head is fuzzy from that familiar lethargic feeling of sitting around with relatives for too long. The sound of the TV in the background is irksome, especially with the last glow of summer still in the air. But for once, I've planned ahead. Before we left I packed a bag with everyone's bathing suit and a change of clothes.

"Why don't we go to the beach?" I ask, using an upbeat voice. Even though I know that Gloria and Leon never step foot in the sand, and certainly wouldn't dream of treading anywhere near the water.

"I don't know," Leon replies, "the sand is uncomfortable."

"The beach?" Gloria sighs. "Wouldn't it be nicer to stay inside in the air conditioning?"

But I'm determined to fight against the stagnation, the sitting around talking about which houses are for sale in the neighborhood. It's a beautiful, warm September day, and there won't be many of these days left. "Come on," I persevere. "Remember how much Eli and Eva loved playing in that playground on the Bradley Beach boardwalk? Eli could ride with Leon in the Miata," I think to add. "And the rest of us can drive in our car."

Roy told me about the Miata just after we met, how he and his brother had bought it for Leon for his sixty-fifth birthday. I'd been impressed by this grand gesture, especially once I met Leon, a man who was far from a roadster and seemed content with his sedentary life. Roy and I borrowed the Miata ourselves a couple of times when we first got together. Once when we drove up to Saratoga with the hood down on an early summer weekend, we ran into an unexpected hail storm and had to quickly bolt the roof back down again. Mostly the car now just sits in the garage, except that Leon gets a thrill out of driving Eli on short rides when we come to visit.

"Let's drive in the Miata!" shrieks Eli.

It works. Gloria finds a couple of extra towels and carefully folds them into an old beach bag.

Once we get there, Eli prefers to stay at the playground on the boardwalk, not wanting to come down to the beach like I had in mind. But Eva and I continue to the water's edge. The waves come rippling in and tickle our feet, and in no time we're playing in the water. Before long, Eli's grown tired of the jungle gym, and he runs down to the water and jumps in, too. We splash around gleefully, and when I try to come out for a rest Eli and Eva pull me back in again.

All covered in salt water and refreshed, I look out at the horizon. The sun glitters everywhere as it reflects off the water. Gloria and Leon are smiling and nodding in appreciation when we reach them back at the boardwalk. "Careful to get that sand off your feet before you put on your sneakers," she says to Eli. "Don't worry," I say, as I rub the kids' feet dry and shake out their shoes.

≈

This Rosh Hashanah is still summer-like. And Roy's friend's house on Fire Island is empty, so he invites us to take it for the weekend. The kids especially love the hot tub. The thermostat's broken so it doesn't get too hot, and they splash around for hours at a time. We walk on the wide, open, beautiful beach, empty and perfectly warm this first weekend in October.

It's getting to be time to take the ferry back home, but first Roy suggests that we take the bagels that are leftover from breakfast and throw them into the water, to rid ourselves of our sins of the year that is ending. I love the idea of celebrating our own version of the custom of throwing our sins away as we think about the year that's passed, and I'm surprised that Roy has thought of it. With our bag of bagels in hand, we lean over the edge of the dock. Eva throws her whole bagel into the bay at once, before she notices that the rest of us are breaking off small pieces.

"For everything sad," I say as I throw a bit of bagel into the water. "And for every time I was angry," I say, flinging in another small piece.

"For every time I yelled at Mom," says Roy. "And for every time I yelled at Eli. For every time I yelled at Eva."

"For every time I was sad," Eli shouts out. "And angry."

Eva begs us to give her more pieces, so she can throw them, too. Eventually all of our crumbs are in the water. "Can we get all the bread back now and eat it?" Eva asks. I don't know if we'll ever do this again, but we've made our own new ritual, and we take the ferry home, feeling complete.

This October 13th is the eighteenth anniversary of Danny's death. I hadn't even noticed the date until a friend, whose brother also committed suicide and who always carefully remembers, calls to say she's thinking of me. On this lovely fall day, I've been busily absorbed in trying to sell a manuscript that I'm excited about, and hadn't been thinking about Danny at all. It's the first time in eighteen years that I haven't noticed what day today is.

When Danny was an adorable, rosy-cheeked baby, I loved how he looked in his light yellow pajamas. On weekend mornings a lot of times I'd get into his crib and play with him. Sometimes Teddy would come in, too. But mostly it was my own little home with Danny, my cuddly human doll. I'd comb his soft, reddish hair and arrange it in different styles with my barrettes. As he got a little older, I helped him learn to stand up by grabbing onto the crib bars. On the long afternoons when I didn't have to go to Boston with my mother to visit Teddy in the hospital, I watched Danny as he learned to crawl and cheered him on when he started walking for the first time by holding onto the furniture.

When I did go with my mother to the hospital to visit Teddy, I couldn't actually see him, because I was too young. I'd wait for my mother in the big waiting room on the lobby floor around the corner from the elevators. My mother would make sure I had a book to read. But mostly I just waited and concentrated on how to spread out the time. I'd choose just the right moment to go into the gift shop with the nickel my mother had given me to buy a Chunky bar. Then, I'd go back to my chair, unfold the silver wrapper, and nibble the milk chocolate block filled with whole peanuts and raisins as slowly as I could, so the time wouldn't seem so long.

I liked knowing that I was close to my mother, even if she was upstairs with the sick patients, where I wasn't allowed to go. And I knew we'd get to drive home together. We'd usually get stuck in rush hour in the big traffic circle in front of the billboard saying, "If You Lived Here, You'd Be Home Now." "That would be nice, to be home now," I'd say. And my mother would explain that it was supposed to be an advertisement for an apartment complex.

During those couple of years when Danny was a baby learning to walk and talk, it was like our family had two locations—the hospital and home. Even though there was something comforting about being with my mother and Teddy in the hospital, I liked it better being in the sunroom in Marblehead with Danny, with the babysitter in the other room. When Danny and I were playing together I wasn't thinking about where we were, or that my mother was somewhere else.

Teddy's being sick with a rare kidney disease set him apart. I'd make cards for him to read in the hospital because sometimes he'd be there for as long as a month or even two months at a time. Sometimes my father would buy a puzzle or a game for me to send to him. "Why don't you give your brother this tic-tac-toe board," my father would say. "Your mother can bring it to him." Or sometimes he'd help me to make a rebus puzzle to send to Teddy.

Teddy's life in the hospital was a mystery, but sometimes I'd get stories. Once when it was an unusually beautiful spring day and Teddy was feeling well, my mother told me that she and my grandmother took him for a walk outside in the garden. Teddy was wearing the red corduroy bathrobe my mother had made for him. Usually, my mother told me, he could only see the garden from his window, but on that day he got to go outside. Once he sent home a brown and yellow tile ashtray that he'd made with the "activity lady," who would come around and play with all the kids who had to stay in their beds. Teddy was part of a special group of children at the hospital who they gave special tests to. They were called "guinea pigs" and he was an especially good "guinea pig." And there was the famous time when my grandmother was visiting and she went with my mother to see Teddy. She got pushed into the broom closet by the Secret Service, she told us, to make room for President Kennedy, who was in the hospital, too, visiting his newborn baby son Patrick. My grandmother's story was very exciting, but then the little baby died and they had a funeral, and the president and Jackie were in the newspaper. It was lucky that Teddy lived.

When I was about nine, my mother thought she'd found a serious health matter for me, too. I was recovering from the grippe and standing in a short nightgown in my parents' bedroom, when my mother noticed that one of my hips looked like it was a little higher than the other. She brought me to the doctor, and sure enough either I had scoliosis or a leg length discrepancy, they weren't sure which. In a matter of weeks, I was going to Children's Hospital, too, to get X-rays of my legs and spine. At the hospital, an exercise therapist taught me to do special exercises. I hadn't yet had my growth spurt, so they weren't sure of what would happen to me, but I was told that if I didn't do the exercises every day, I might have to wear a special body brace, or even worse than that—a body cast. In fear, I did the exercises almost every day—leg lifts and standing up pushups with my hands pressed against the corner of two walls. And for the next few years, I'd go to the hospital every six months for X-rays and a check-up. It was determined that I had a "young bone age" and my growth spurt would probably come late, so I had to keep up with the daily exercises.

When we first moved to Connecticut, we'd make occasional trips back to Boston to the hospital for checkups. But eventually we switched to a more convenient hospital in Hartford, where I'd get X-rays and be examined by a different doctor. The new doctor said I'd now need to wear a lift in my shoe, with my ever-approaching growth spurt still to come. My mother brought my shoes to a shoemaker to have the lift put in, like the doctor had instructed. He'd promised me the lift wouldn't show. But the shoes came back looking ugly, and the lift *did* show. No one in Boston had ever mentioned anything about special shoes. I refused to wear them and nothing much seemed to go wrong. Later, I discovered that nearly half the population has a leg length discrepancy.

I don't think my mother ever found a special illness for Danny, although there was once some talk of his having a deviated septum. One thing that made him a little different from the rest of the family, and maybe a little more delicate, was that he was prone to sunburn. Once when he was about six or seven, he went to the beach with a friend and came home with a really bad burn. I covered him with sour cream, having read somewhere that this was a good antidote. Then I sliced some cucumbers and put them on top of the sour cream, thinking they might help to cool him off.

We all adored Danny. We would do anything for him. I remember him wearing his bright blue Captain Kangaroo hat, a small molded plastic version of the one Captain Kangaroo wore on TV. He loved it so much he chewed a hole in it. And he wore it every day, even in the summer when it made his head sweat. One long car trip, probably on the way to New York or Washington, it flew out the window into the middle of the highway. My father actually pulled the car over, and got out and ran along the shoulder of the road, cars rushing by as he tried to catch up with the small blue hat that was blowing backwards. But he couldn't get it back. It took a while to adjust to seeing Danny's head without his hat.

Another time, it was a summer evening and it was unusual because we all went out for dinner at a restaurant. We were sitting at a big round table at Doane's, a seafood place on the water, and we were right in the center of the restaurant. Danny still had to sit on a booster seat, and I remember him happily smiling, perched up higher than the rest of us, like a little king on his throne. My mother helped me and Teddy look at the menu, skipping over all the fried clams and shrimp, which weren't kosher, until we found the fish & chips and salmon croquettes. Just as the food came, I noticed a yellow pool on the floor around Danny's chair. He was just sitting there smiling in his booster seat. I whispered that Danny had peed all over the floor, and my mother said we should just eat quickly, which we did. My father paid and we huddled out of the restaurant together, Danny still smiling, and nobody was angry at all. When Danny was a baby there was nothing wrong with him. And sometimes there was nothing wrong with our family either.

≈

My aunt Helene has made a sculpture in memory of my mother. Not only for my mother, but also in honor of all the family members who have died in the past two decades—Danny, Joe, Cecile, and most recently my cousin's new baby who died at birth. Helene thought it would be a beautiful gift to place outside the Hebrew school that my mother led for so many years. Helene's bronze sculptures have been commissioned by parks and other outdoor public spaces all around Washington, DC, and the Hebrew school where my mother had presided was pleased to be the recipient of this new work. "They want to have a special commemorative ceremony at the Temple," my father told Ted and me.

My father has been consumed by planning this service to honor my mother. For months, he's been consulting with family members over potential dates, persistently asking Ted and me and Nate to deliver speeches, and checking with us about last-minute additions to the invitation list. It's difficult to understand the degree of my father's dedication to this event. I've tried to stay away from his attempts to rope us into his plans, and so has Ted. "Look," Ted told him, "go ahead and make the plans. Make whatever speech you want. We'll come, but you organize it." For years, the family (including my father) rolled our eyes when my mother would describe the minutiae of her Hebrew school world. But ever since her death, my father's become enamored of my mother's stature as a Jewish educator.

It's a cold, rainy weekend when we drive up to Boston. I'm tired of my family's preoccupation with death and depression that seems so out of proportion. "Don't you think it's strange," I commented to Ted when I first heard about the ceremony, "to have the sculpture be in honor of a barely born baby?" But Ted thought I was being intolerant. After all, the baby was Helene's grandchild, he said reasonably.

My father has invited all the relatives and my mother's closest friends to come back to his house for a meal after the ceremony at the Hebrew school. At first, he was going to have it catered, but then he decided he would handle it on his own. Had I been paying more attention, I might have intruded earlier, but now it dawns on me that my father pulling this whole thing off on his own is going to be impossible. I tell Roy maybe we better go up early, in case he needs some help.

The four of us drive up to Ted's house in Connecticut for lunch the day before. My father meets us there, and then we accompany him back up to Andover—Roy and the kids in our car, and me and my father in his. On the way, we stop in Brookline at the delicatessen to pick up the bagels for the next day. "How many people were you expecting?" I realize I have no idea how many people he's invited. "Forty," he answers, "about forty."

"We'll need sixty bagels," I tell the man behind the counter, "an assortment."

"No!" My father is suddenly panicked. "I don't actually think there will be forty people."

"OK," I say. "How many bagels do you want to get?"

"Three dozen, three dozen plain bagels," he yells out to the man.

"Why all plain?" I ask.

"I think that's what most people like to eat."

I can't figure out his logic. The rest of the family is sitting in the car waiting for us to buy the bagels, and I have no choice but to take over.

"Eight poppy, half a dozen sesame, half a dozen everything, a dozen plain . . ." I tell the man, who's standing there, waiting for us to decide what we want.

"How about cream cheese?" I try to defer to my father.

"I have some cheeses and spreads at home," my father says. But as I imagine what his refrigerator might really have in it, I ignore him. "People are bringing pastries," he tries to tell me.

"Four pounds of cream cheese," I say to the man. "And lox, we'll need lox. Four pounds of nova." I'm treating my father like a child, an insignificant child—not a child of my own. "You can always freeze the leftovers," I instruct him. I sound like my mother.

Once we get back to the house, I see signs that he's been attempting to organize a party. On the dining room table is a stack of about twenty-five small-sized plastic plates, for people to put their pastries on, he says. He's also purchased three fake cut-glass plastic platters to hold the pastries, and some doilies for decoration. It reminds me of the time when Teddy and I were about five and seven, and decided to give my parents a surprise party one summer afternoon and serve ice cream sodas. We set the picnic table in the backyard, excited to start drinking the concoctions we'd made. Much to our disappointment, none of the guests we tried to invite on a half hour's notice could come. So we opened the box of colored paper straws, and sipped down the ice cream sodas ourselves. But Teddy and I were children. My father is seventy-five years old.

I tell myself that I shouldn't be surprised by my father's oblivious behavior. But it's hard not to be angry at him. Hadn't he paid any attention over all the years when my mother served all kinds of meals for all kinds of festivities and family gatherings? The buffet drawers in the dining room and the kitchen cabinets are still filled with platters and bowls, and serving spoons, forks, and tongs of all shapes and sizes. How could he have chosen to buy plastic serving trays that we

didn't need, when he hadn't even considered how he was going to feed the guests? He had invited at least forty people to
put down their schedules and travel to the event he'd planned,
and all he could manage was a doll's version of a party. How
could he possibly remain so unaware of my mother as the responsible head of our household on a daily basis? It took effort
and planning to keep the family organized the way my mother
did. Now he has a new adoration of my mother as a Jewish
educator, but it's as if he has no idea at all who she really was.

In the refrigerator, there are some more faint signs of
thought. One bottle of Coke, one of ginger ale, and sure
enough a couple of pre-packaged cheese spreads. I angrily
make my shopping list for the morning: soda, seltzer, juice
and milk for the kids, fruit, butter, napkins . . .

In Ted's old bedroom, I can't sleep. I nudge Roy to go and
check on the kids, who are in my old room. He tells me they're
sleeping and dozes off again himself. I try to breathe myself
into some degree of calmness, but the mattress is old and uncomfortable and the sheets are frayed. As the bed creaks and
the hours pass, my father's lack of hospitality becomes excruciating. By dawn I'm completely exhausted.

Everyone's still in bed when I go downstairs in the morning, except for my father who is standing in the living room
waiting for me. His sad eyes dispel my aggravation. It looks
like he's been awake for a while. On the arm of the couch I notice a worn-looking piece of paper with the words that must be
his speech written out on it. I realize that he's been rehearsing.

We don't have breakfast, but go right out into the cold
drizzle and drive to the grocery store. In the daylight, gray as
it is, the situation seems more manageable. My father and I
comb through the aisles of the store, me reading from my list,

my father fetching what he can. We drive home again, and still he doesn't mention anything, about how he got us into this whirlwind, or about his being thankful for my last-minute help. I think back to the time when he told me about how deeply concerned he was over Ted when he was splitting up with his girlfriend and how he wished he could help him. "Tell him you love him and that you're there for him," I tried to offer some basic advice. He looked at me blankly. "I already did," he said. "I told him that once this was behind him, everything would be fine." "But did you tell him you love him?" I repeated. He just plain didn't understand what I was saying. His vocabulary has always been his own.

At the ceremony, my father says the words he'd been practicing. He delivers a lovely speech, honoring my mother in a way he wasn't able to do at her funeral when he didn't have the strength. Helene speaks about the sculpture she's made, about its themes of death and life, and about my mother and our family. The rabbis praise my mother's contribution to Jewish education. Most of the relatives have come. And there are a number of parents from the school there, too. Even some of the children my mother once taught have come to show their appreciation. After the service, we all go out into the cold dampness and gather around the entrance that leads to the Hebrew school. My father undrapes Helene's bronze sculpture, the image of a grandfather dancing festively and holding a menorah up high with his grandchildren perched on his arms and at his feet, a dream symbol of a happy Jewish family fortified by tradition.

The rain is driving down heavily when we reach Andover. And the sight of my father's house is actually almost an oasis. My mother's friends are already inside, and they've set up heaping plates of pastries that they've baked for the occasion. Together we arrange the table and manage to give it a sense of bounty. People seem grateful and nourished. I marvel that the occasion has actually turned out alright. My mother has been recognized for her achievements, and my father, who looks gratified, may now be able to leave a portion of his mourning behind him.

Eleven

E ven when I was small, when my father said things like, "You have to do it because I say so!" in a stern voice, it made me laugh because it was hard to take it seriously that he was really in charge. In some ways, I guess he *was* in charge because no one ever thought to say no to him when we were dragged around from state to state, and school to school, because it was time for him to change his job again. When he couldn't get along with his boss, I thought he must be strong for standing up for his ideals. When we'd hear him talking disparagingly about the company managers at the dinner table, we just figured he was right, even though it could mean uprooting the whole family yet again. I even saw the humor in it, maybe because it ran so straight against my mother's anxious concern that everything be safe and normal.

My father's haphazard ways made us laugh. One of his roles was taking care of the cars. And even though it could be frustrating when they wouldn't start, and he'd blame the faulty carburetor or alternator that hadn't been fixed right after he'd just taken it to be repaired at Kmart the week before, there was something comical about the way he'd manage to keep the cars just barely functioning, just enough to get us where we were going. He'd fail to replace bald tires even when we went on ski trips and we'd risk driving off of a slippery cliff on the icy roads, or he wouldn't fill the car with gas in time and we'd run out before we got where we were going. He'd matter-of-factly leave us all waiting in the car on the side of the highway, until he'd eventually appear again, jogging toward us with rusty gas can in hand from the nearest service station. He was hardly the model of a responsible father.

Sometimes when he'd push things too far, it would clearly be at the family's expense, like the time he passed an undercover police car on a double line, when we were driving home from a day of skiing. "Joel, what on earth are you doing?" my mother screamed, as the police turned on his siren and pulled us over. We then had to follow the police back to the station, and wait in the cold while my father was inside being interrogated. My mother yelled at him the whole way home, but we didn't really pay attention because to the three of us it was another good story about my father to tell our friends. His negligence, while frustrating, could somehow be turned into an endearing trait.

When my father visits us in New York, Roy and I usually go out on Saturday night and my father babysits, like both my parents used to do together before my mother died. But this is the weekend of Eli's seventh birthday, and we're all staying home on Saturday night so I can make Eli's big chocolate cake for tomorrow, along with the thirty cupcakes that need to be baked, frosted, and delivered to his class on Monday morning. I'll need to get up early to prepare all of the party bags and decorations, before we go to the Planetarium where we'll meet up with the seven boys who Eli has invited to his party. Roy decides to go to bed early because he thinks he's coming down with a cold. So it's just me baking in the kitchen, while my father reads a book in the living room.

"Do you need any help, Annie?" my father asks. I notice that he's edged his chair into the kitchen, and is watching my every-baking-action. His obliviousness to boundaries really gets on my nerves, but as I glance at the clock and realize that it's already past ten, there's no time to be annoyed. I'm about to run out of cupcake papers and I still have the third batch left to bake. "Dad, would you mind running out for some cupcake papers? West Side Market is just a couple of blocks down Broadway on the east side of the street, and they'll definitely have some."

"Sure, Annie," he says, happy to be of assistance. And off he goes.

At about eleven o'clock, it's been more than an hour and I realize my father's still not back. Once the second batch of cupcakes is out of the oven, I decide I'd better go out to look for him. I walk slowly and scan the streets along my way, not wanting to miss him in transit. I get all the way to the market, and there's my father standing in the middle of the baking products aisle, raising his arm to greet me with a package of cupcake papers in hand. "I *found* them," he says, apparently unaware of the fact that I've left the kitchen to come find *him*. I wonder why after all this time he hasn't asked anyone for help, but I don't bother to mention it. We walk home together, I finish the final batch of cupcakes and collapse into bed.

The next morning I'm up early to finish the frosting and decorating, so I can get the kids bathed, and we can make it to the Planetarium on time. I've just finished with the party bags, when Roy says, "Why don't I stay here and get everything ready while you go to the Planetarium?" I can't believe it. Just what can he possibly have in mind—dialing the phone to order a pizza before we get back, while I bring seven boys plus Eli and Eva and my father to the star show? "*No!*" I shout back. But then I can only think that maybe his cold is really bad if he's come up with this idea, and I relent. We leave Roy behind and rush off to find a cab.

The boys arrive in the museum foyer and the activity level quickly mounts as they wrestle and throw each other around on the floor. Eva grabs onto me for protection, and my father is off looking at something. Our babysitter's supposed to be meeting us to help out, but she hasn't shown up.

Finally we're all sitting in our seats, ready to watch the star show, which much to my relief will last a full fifteen minutes. The boys *love* it, their awe palpable as we travel through a facsimile of a black hole. But then it's over, and it's time to coordinate our exit. The boys are all banging on the big bronze Neptune like it's a drum. I shoo them away from the planet and then they're all together jumping on a scale that will tell them how much they would weigh on Jupiter. We get out of the museum, I hail three cabs for our excursion home, and we manage to all make it back to the apartment, where the pizza is waiting for us, along with the cake. A new computer game mesmerizes the boys. I take a seat by myself at the end of the table, and bite into a big piece of chocolate birthday cake. I try to amuse myself with the thought that the act of giving birth to Eli seven years ago was possibly more intense than this birthday party.

Once the apartment is cleared out of all the seven-year-olds except for Eli, it's time for my father to leave, too. As he steps into the elevator, he advises me, "You should give Roy a hug," he says. "You know, he's not feeling well." I stifle my exasperation, and usher my father into the elevator.

~~

"Please don't say that Mary Tyler Moore is exactly like Mom," Ted said when I called to ask him if he'd seen *Ordinary People* yet. But clearly he agreed. "You're determined, Beth, but you're not strong," he quoted back Donald Sutherland's line, already having memorized it. Donald Sutherland was the father and Mary Tyler Moore played Beth, the mother. "She's exactly like Mom," we agreed. And that was even before Danny had committed suicide, just like Mary Tyler Moore's son attempted to do in the movie, after the drowning of his brother before him. That was when my mother's compulsion for normalcy seemed at its most oppressive, after we already knew the truth about my grandfather but before it was completely clear that her construction of life couldn't hold anymore.

Only now do I begin to understand my mother's endurance from a different perspective, her drive to impose a sense of order on her family. Just like Mary Tyler Moore in the movie, my mother worked hard to keep up appearances. But maybe that was more heroic than I'd given her credit for. In what must have been my mother's version of a normal family, my father had to function in the role of protector and my mother as his wife. It must have been important to my mother that my father be in charge, even if all she could get was my father's oblivious form of that. If he could appear to be at the helm, then we would look like a normal family, and maybe then we would be one. My mother made sure that it was my father who made the big decisions, like where he would work, and where we would live, and how much we could afford to spend on a house or a vacation. Also on her list of my father's charges must have been filling up the car with gas. Even when the needle was so often so close to empty, and even though my mother could easily have made the occasional extra stop at the gas station herself, she opted for anxiety rather than filling the car up with gas, and eventually we'd feel that familiar chugging motion of the car that told us the inevitable—that she'd have to call my father at work and yell at him because again we'd run out of gas.

Other than the jobs that were allotted to my father, everything else was my mother's domain. Her role of family organizer may not have made her happy, and often it made her unlikable, especially compared to my father, who could be viewed as sensitive and quirky, more like a child, more like me. But while she may not have always been popular at home, she also refused to be a martyr and she found herself a different venue where she could be appreciated in her role. In the Hebrew school, she found a place where she could reap unqualified praise for her work. While I'm sure she would have preferred that her family didn't belittle the work she did there, she didn't let that get in her way.

My mother and I were completely different, something I asserted whenever anyone tried to compare us. Yes, we both had curly hair, but mine was thicker and hers was darker. She had a round face, and I had an oval one. She had broad shoulders and I didn't. I resembled my father. I had his same nose, his eyes, and his narrow build. And of course, the biggest difference between my mother and me was that she had no sensitivity, or at least no sensitivity to me. My mother was driven and she squelched emotion, and I was questioning, often with questions that my mother would have preferred to remain unasked.

But now with the distance of having her beside me, I can acknowledge that my mother did have her strength. She found a way to do much more than survive. She endured. And she did this with a family legacy that when seen from the outside could only be considered of tragic proportion—surrounded by suicide on all sides. In her own way, she would only accept progress for the next generation, and in her own way she achieved that. Her father had only made it to age fifty when he'd committed suicide by taking too many pills and was found dead in a men's bath on the Lower East Side. My mother had lived to age sixty-eight, and when she died it was accidentally, all the way on the other side of the world, in the beauty of the Great Barrier Reef, under a big, blue sky, with fish all around. Ultimately, the end of her life seemed more like a story of death than the actuality of gory details, a death that would always remain distant and a little unknown. Maybe that's what she had been trying to pass down to her children—a story. Maybe that's what she was doing when she so persistently veered away from the truth. Maybe a story of her life was the best inheritance she could offer.

≈

My father has finally agreed to invite Judith to his seventy-fifth birthday dinner. "You've been close friends for almost three years now," I'd pushed him. "It's a good time to be inclusive,"

Ted tried, too. "You've been to all of Judith's family events. Now it's time to invite her to ours." And finally my father has agreed. Eva has heard my father mention Judith once or twice, and she's intrigued. "Will she be like my grandmother?" she wants to know. "Sort of," I say. "She's Papa Joel's friend and she's really nice. Maybe next time when he comes to New York, she'll come with him and they can babysit together."

Ted has reserved a table for the six of us—him and Janet, me and Roy, and my father and Judith—at a new restaurant in Boston. It's a place with white tablecloths and shiny silverware, maybe a little too stiff for us. It's hard not to think of my father's sixty-fifth birthday when we gathered at another Boston restaurant. That was ten years before, when my mother had been strongly present, and Roy had been only a recent addition. My father orders the foie gras as an appetizer, followed by chicken rolled up with brie. "Don't you think that's a little high in cholesterol?" Roy whispers to me. But my father, now seventy-five, eats with gusto. "This is the best food I've ever tasted," he says. After dessert, Ted takes a picture to remember the occasion.

The next day, we visit my father in Andover. With the passage of time, the house has become more wanting. It's clear that my father hasn't spent much time here lately. Eli asks if I can make him a cup of tea, and I find a teabag in the otherwise empty cabinets. My father has already brought the gallon of milk up from the freezer. "It will thaw in a few minutes," he says. I brew the tea lightly, the way Eli likes it, and add the milk, picking out the flecks of ice floating on top. The honey's hardened and I can't spoon it out of the bottle, so I use sugar instead. "It tastes funny, Mom," Eli says. "I don't want to drink it." I tell him we'll make a new cup when we get home.

≈

With Gloria's declining condition, we couldn't plan ahead, we were lucky to get a last-minute flight to San Juan for Presidents' Day Weekend. And Roy successfully found a Puerto Rican family resort on the internet with reservations available. The swimming pool is especially designed for kids—three feet deep at both ends. Eli and Eva jump right in, happy to be free at last.

Roy and I survey the premises. The beach is a little disappointing, the sand coarser than other Caribbean beaches we've been to. But at least we're in a tropical place. I'm hoping that the salve of the water and sun will get under Roy's skin, and mine, too, and that we'll all feel far away from the gray February we've been inhabiting.

"Look Mom, over there! That's where Jesus lived." Eva points to a thatched gazebo on the beach. I wonder what she could possibly be talking about.

"Jesus?" I say. "I don't know. Maybe."

"He died on a post, right?" says Eva. Her pre-school teacher had already asked me gently to ask Eva not to keep telling her classmates that Santa Claus was really a man dressed in a costume.

Then I remember Eli and Eva arguing last week in the bathtub. "Is it true?" Eli had wanted to know. "Eva's friend said that Jesus died on a post. That's not true is it?"

"Well, yes it is," I had answered.

"Told you!" said Eva.

"Do you really believe there was someone named Jesus?" Eli asked me.

"Yes, I believe there was a man named Jesus."

"And he died on a post," chimed in Eva. "He was nailed there. And he couldn't have anything to eat."

"Mom, do you believe Jesus was God?" Eli wanted to know.

"No, I believe he was a man, and I believe he died on a post. But I don't believe he was God."

"That's ridiculous that people think he was God," asserted Eli, who next to Roy has become the family's greatest pragmatist.

"He died on a post," Eva says kicking sand on the beach. "Come on, Mom. Let's go look for the post where he died."

Twelve

"Gloria has been put on oxygen." Roy's voice is stoic, but his eyes show his pain. He hangs up the phone and says he's going to go out to buy the newspaper. He doesn't want to talk about it. "We have to tell the kids," I say. We'd decided not to point out Gloria's illness until it was really obvious, figuring they wouldn't grasp the notion of so much time passing before the inevitable end of her life would finally take place.

Our plan was to stop in New Jersey on our way to Washington for Nate and Gail's daughter Erica's bat mitzvah. We would visit Gloria and Leon for an hour or so, long enough for Eli and Eva to see Gloria, and for us to explain that she has cancer.

I call Gloria to tell her we're on our way, and Eli grabs the phone from my hand. "I know you have a tube in your nose," he states plainly. "And that you have cancer." Roy must have explained about Gloria while I was in the shower. I take the phone back. "I'll tell them anything they want to ask me," she says to me, bold and straightforward.

On the way to New Jersey, the kids are quiet. When we arrive, Gloria's sitting on the living room couch with her new breathing apparatus. I give her a hug, but the kids keep their distance. They play in the den with Leon and watch TV while Roy and I sit with Gloria in the living room. The truth is that despite the machinery the oxygen makes her look more healthy and comfortable than she did the last visit. The kids drift back in to check out the respirator. When it's time to leave, they beg Gloria for candy just like they always do. And of course she gives each of them a big handful of Hershey's Kisses to take with them for the ride to DC. We get back into the car and continue on our way. No one mentions Gloria, but Roy seems relieved. The kids stay quiet. There are none of their usual speculations about the mystery of death and illness. "Can you die if you bend your finger back really far? How about if you break your leg?" It's as though those questions are now off limits.

~

When I leave for London for the book fair, I'm overwhelmed by sadness when I say goodbye to the kids and Roy. The last time I'd made this trip, I was nearly euphoric as my flight left the ground. It was the first time I'd left the country since the kids were born, and it was as if my identity shifted in midair. I changed from a mother who also had a career as a literary agent, into a free spirit flying away. It had been a thrill to travel alone across the ocean. I'd prepared in advance, scavenging out my old copy of London A-Z, making sure I had plenty of client lists on hand, and multiple copies of my fully-booked schedule of meetings with publishers, just in case I happened to lose a copy.

This year I'm disorganized. When I arrive at my hotel and unpack, I realize that I've forgotten my business cards. And I've left the melatonin tablets at home, the ones I so carefully packed last year to help avoid jet lag so I'd be able to keep functioning at a good pace. I read a few pages of a novel until it's late enough to go to sleep. I think of Eli and Eva playing at home and my eyes well up. My life at home with my husband and two children suddenly seems perfect, even though we all argued while I was packing my bags to leave. That had been twelve hours ago, the beginning of this very long day. Now it's time to go to sleep here, while there the day is almost about to begin. I feel too far away.

The trip turns out to be productive, even if it's not as exciting as the first time. I get swept up in the busyness of the fair. The foreign editors I meet seem to be interested in my clients' books, so I can count the trip as a success. When it's time to leave, I'm efficient and have everything packed before I go to bed. I'll be ready for my six o'clock wake-up call in the morning. All I have to do is get dressed and make it to the airport with the necessary two hours to spare.

On the train to Heathrow, I have that same sad feeling I had on the way here. I notice a girl sitting across from me. She's about twenty, and slightly genderless, and for some reason she reminds me a little of Danny. It strikes me at this moment, how the lengths of people's lives are so variable. Danny had a short life, too short to qualify as fulfilled. My mother's was medium to long, but much longer than Danny's. My great-grandmother, maybe the only member of my family who had a really long life, died at 104, and because of that everyone came to admire her and laughed about how she'd survived all those years living on black instant coffee and pickled herring.

The flight turns out to be more than an hour late, so there's plenty of time to waste at the airport. I buy a cup of coffee so that I can legitimately sit at a café table and read my book. The coffee tastes like it's been sitting in a big vat. As I add some extra milk, it dawns on me that I don't know where the milk comes from. There's been a lot of talk about mad cow disease this year, although the word is that it's just a lot of exaggeration by foreigners. But suddenly I'm very worried about death. Milk comes from cows, I reason, so maybe it's harmful just like the meat. Maybe all of the milk I've been drinking in my coffee on this trip will make me die in fifteen years. If that happened, I'd be younger than my mother when she died.

Finally I settle into my seat on the plane, seatbelt on and ready to go. The couple in the seat behind me is loudly grabbing at the radio and movie controls and the woman keeps on kicking my seat, but I figure I'll fall asleep soon and it won't matter. When I turn around to see whether they might be quieting down, incredibly I see there are two men in uniform standing next to them. "We're asking you to leave the plane now," one of them is saying. "We're arresting you." The couple gathers up their things and leaves with the officials. They don't resist at all. After they exit, the official men return to search the overhead bins and under the seats, apparently looking for dangerous substances. They don't find anything. But there's an announcement saying that we'll be a bit more delayed while the luggage of the two departing passengers is removed from under the plane.

I sit back in my seat and close my eyes, feeling oddly secure at the elimination of the danger I hadn't known was there. When I arrive at JFK, I call Roy and tell him why I'd been delayed, the story of the arrest in the seat behind me. "You're lucky to be safe," he says with relief in his voice. "Your life might have been at risk." Strangely, that was a possibility I hadn't considered. My perspective on death and risk is a little out of kilter, I now know enough to realize.

The cab ride home is quick, and I'm already at home to greet the kids when they return from school. The moment I see their faces at the door, I know exactly why I've been away. It's so I can come back and see them again. After only six days they each appear to have miraculously changed. "Next year we want to come to London," Eva says. They tear through my bags looking for the Cadbury chocolate bars and the trinkets I've brought them. Eli looks inexplicably tall, his new adult teeth decidedly longer. And Eva has arranged her hair in three pigtails. She stares right into my eyes, as if to be sure I'm really there. I can barely believe that this beautiful being who now almost reaches my waist is truly my daughter. The week-long separation from the everyday now seems all the more unbearable.

"We visit Gloria and Leon *every* weekend," the kids say. "There's nothing for us to do there. We don't want to go." Despite their logic, Roy is offended, and he can't cover it up. "It means a lot to Gloria when you visit," he says. "And it means a lot to me, too. She's very sick now." The report is that Gloria's condition has declined significantly in the past few days. The hospice aid, who now visits regularly, says that maybe the cancer is getting into her brain, while the family doctor says he thinks it's the high level of morphine that's affecting her thought processes. Roy and I have already decided that it's important to bring the kids on our visit to see Gloria today. Before she gets even sicker, before she dies.

"Dad can go by himself," Eli says. "We want to stay home. We want to play with our friends." I promise them a trip to the playground near the beach when we get there. This makes Eva happy, but it's not enough for Eli. I promise them some surprise treat, maybe the delicious flying saucer ice cream sandwiches they sell near the beach.

Still resisting, they get into the car, and refuse to fall asleep like they usually do, even though they were up very late last night and woke up very early this morning. When we arrive, it's time for lunch and there's no food in the house so the first thing we do is order a pizza. Then we go in to see Gloria, who's now stationed in the den on her oxygen machine. I'm shocked to see how drastically she's changed. It's been three weeks since I've seen her, but Roy visited just last weekend when I was in London and he looks shaken by the sight of her, too. The muscles around her mouth don't seem to work quite right. The ends of her lips droop down. Her eyes keep closing, like she's fading away. "How's your sister?" she asks me. "Is she still sick?" Obviously, I've never had a sister. I look at Roy to confirm what she could possibly mean. I see the tears creeping down Roy's face. He tries to keep from showing his emotions to Gloria. But in a moment she will forget what she sees anyway. "My short term memory is going," she tells us. "But it will come back." We nod at her, knowing that it won't come back. She seems to understand our words, but can't remember them long enough to answer us. She can no longer have a conversation or read a book, no longer able to remember the preceding sentence. She notices the kids, but can't hold onto her thoughts long enough to talk to them.

When the pizza arrives, I sit and eat with Eli and Eva at the dining room table, while Roy stays in the den with Gloria and Leon. "Why isn't Gloria eating with us?" they want to know. They seem not to see what's in front of us. I explain that Gloria is too weak to come to the table. "She can't breathe," says Eva. "That's why she needs that machine. She'll need it until she gets better."

"Yes," agrees Roy, as he comes to join us at the table.

Leon and I take the kids to the playground at the beach, and leave Roy alone with Gloria. We sit on a bench, watching Eli and Eva climb up the slide. They race up and down, and even hold each other's hands, like a model brother and sister. Leon's face looks old, and sadder than I've ever seen him. A few stray pieces of his white hair blow in the chilly March breeze. His eyes are blue, not as pale as Roy's, but the same sensitive eyes. And like Roy, he cries easily, sentimental at heart despite the rational exterior. Leon tearfully tells me how Gloria has become uncharacteristically docile over the past months. But in the last couple of days she's taken a different turn, refusing to swallow her medication; she physically pushes him away and spits out the pills. It's her way of preparing to die, the hospice aid explained to Leon. Whether this is because she thinks the medicine doesn't matter anymore, or whether it's her way of rebelling against the inevitable, no one seems to know. But it means she will die soon.

Leon says that he's looking into getting twenty-four-hour at-home care. Eight-hour care is another possibility, but he doesn't think that's enough. He's no longer able to care for Gloria on his own, he tells me, not physically or emotionally. The hospice people are helping him to find the right caregiver. Leon's eyes are now streaming.

We're shivering and we can't hold out any longer. I ask the kids if they want to get ice cream. "Yay, ice cream!" they shriek. At the ice cream stand, we all pick out our flying saucers, and we get some extra ones to bring back to Gloria. Back at the house Roy is sitting with Gloria on the couch. She's unbelievably thin, her arms like two long white bones. She reaches out to take one of the flying saucers, and licks it with relish.

I look out the window to check on the kids, and see them trying to play jump rope on the front lawn. They laugh hysterically when they fail, rolling on the ground in giddiness and exhaustion. They're a depiction of children playing. Someday, they'll be us and we'll be old. And someday even further away, and more unbearably, they'll be sick and old and maybe their children will be tending them.

Once we get back home again, we explain to the kids that Gloria is so sick that she may never get well again. "Can we catch what she has?" they want to know. "No," we assure them. "Will she be like this?" asks Eli, reclining on the couch with his arms stretched out and his tongue hanging out of his mouth, his eyes closed tight. "It's not nice to joke about that," says Eva, suddenly serious. Finally, Eli asks the unaskable. "Will she die?"

"Yes," Roy and I say in unison.

"She will probably die from this," one of us repeats.

Thirteen

Eli and I are loading the groceries into the trunk. "Is Leon OK?" he asks me. I remember when my mother died and the child psychologist had stressed the need to focus on the presence of the other living grandparent. I assure him that Leon is fine, and that he's taking care of Gloria. "Soon I won't have anymore grandmothers," Eli says. "It will be like with Papa Joel. I'll only have grandfathers." He asks me whether I think Gloria will definitely die from the cancer. I tell him, "Yes, because it's a cancer that has already spread through her body, and her body is old so it can't fight the cancer.

"Do you think she'll live for a year?" Eli wants to know.

"I don't think so."

"How long?" He's focused now.

"I don't know. Maybe a month."

"Maybe more?" he bargains.

"Maybe," I say. "But not much more. Her body is very weak. Maybe less."

Gloria has been taken to the hospice, her wish to die at home overridden by Leon's anxiety about being her physical and emotional caregiver. He tried the around-the-clock nurse, but it hadn't worked out. Leon was just too overwhelmed by Gloria's descent. She has completely stopped speaking. We think it's because she's furious about being moved out of her home, or maybe she's just plain angry that her body will no longer allow her to communicate. She keeps her lips tightly closed. Her stiff body expresses her overt opposition.

Roy thinks that the move to the hospice will make Gloria shut down more quickly. Based on our uninformed calculations, we'd been predicting that Gloria had two or three more weeks of life. But now, Roy says he thinks it's down to one week.

"Gloria will die soon," I tell the kids again at dinner.

"In a month?" Eli asks again.

"I don't know," I say. "Maybe less."

"Maybe a couple of weeks," Roy says.

"Death is part of life," Eli states too wisely for a seven-year-old. "It's OK because death is part of life." I've noticed that this is becoming Eli's new mantra.

"It is," I agree. "It's a sad part of life. It's especially sad for the people who lose the person who's dying."

"But it's part of life," Eli repeats again. "I know how you feel, Dad," he says to Roy. "You having your mother die is like it would be for me if you died. Only it would be worse for me because you can take care of yourself and I can't." His speech seems almost canned. "My friend James is very scared of dying," he continues. "But I tell him not to be afraid. He won't die until he's very old. Not for a very long time." Roy and I nod at Eli, some kind of miniature soothsayer.

Roy's been visiting Gloria at the hospice every day since she arrived there three days ago. I haven't seen her for almost two weeks, but when we visit her today she doesn't look that different than when I last saw her at the house. She's just thinner. The worst part is that she's entirely unable to express herself with words. She sleeps most of the time except when you hold her hand and talk to her. Then she opens her eyes and moves her head and mouth as though trying to respond, but she can't make her body cooperate. When she rests, breathing through her wide-opened mouth, she looks beautiful, her skin translucent, her body purely existing. If this is truly one step away from death, it's remarkable how close it is to life.

The hospice is an enlightened place, not at all what I imagined for a home for people in the last days of their lives. I've never seen anyone just as they're about to die until now. With my brother, I only saw his body after he died. When my aunt Cecile died of cancer over the course of a few months, I'd never managed to get myself to the hospital to see her during the final weeks of her life. I must have been too afraid to watch. In the case of my mother, the physical reality of her death remains completely in my imagination. But the hospice isn't frightening at all. It's a calm shelter where the hospice workers shepherd people to another world, and they do it knowingly and kindly.

The next day, when Roy calls me from work to tell me that Gloria has just died, for some reason I'm completely surprised.

In the evening, Roy goes down to the Jersey shore to be with his father and his brothers, and I take the kids out to dinner. I let them have anything they want—soda with their meal *and* dessert afterwards. We talk about going to the cemetery the day after tomorrow. There's just going to be a simple burial, nothing ceremonial.

"Will they take Gloria's brain out?" asks Eli.

It takes me a minute to realize he's talking about Egyptian funeral rites. "No," I assure him. "Definitely not. They only did that a very long time ago in Egypt."

Eva asks, "Will we make Gloria's body into art?" For a few moments, I'm puzzled by her question, too. But then she asks me again. "Will we be able to put art on Gloria's body?" she wants to know. And I get that she's still talking about the Egyptians.

"They did that with mummies a long time ago, but not anymore." I try to explain without smiling too much. I know that Eva could really get involved in what Gloria wears when she's buried. I'm sure she'd suggest exotic jewels and other artistic touches. I don't know if she'd approve of Leon's choice to dress Gloria in the denim skirt and jacket that was her favorite.

I sort through my emails, trying to create order before our trip to Jersey for Gloria's funeral the next day. At about 12:30 p.m., I pick up the ringing phone, and hear Eli's little voice at the other end. The school allows the kids to call home from time to time, usually to report on some small ache or pain that the nurse has already deemed unimportant. On the occasions when Eli calls, I can never quite believe it. The image of him picking up the phone and taking charge of his own life always makes me laugh a little. But today his voice is very solemn, and I know it's something serious.

"It's Eli. I don't feel well," he says. "My stomach hurts, Mom. And I have a headache. I can't concentrate."

"Try to stay at school a little longer," I say, "and see how you feel." I hang up, and start to clean off my desk so I can go to the school to pick him up. In a few minutes, he calls again.

"OK. I'll take a cab right over," I promise.

By the time I get to the school, Eli is already on his way out the front door with a teacher, who's taking him to get ice cream. "You take me, Mom," he greets me in a sad voice. The teacher explains that she's been suggesting that Eli think of happy times he's had with his grandmother, but he says he doesn't want to. He says it makes him too sad. I take his hand and we go together in search of the ice cream. As we turn onto First Avenue, Eli explains to me it's a flying saucer ice cream that he's looking for. And I can't help it, I start crying, too. We're never going to find the flying saucer just walking around on First Avenue, so I suggest that we go back to the school to get some better directions. But Eli doesn't want to go back. "What's wrong?" I ask. "What's wrong with going back into the school? We need to pick up your things, anyway."

"I'm too sad," he tells me. "If someone asks me why I'm sad, I don't want to lie. I tell them that my grandmother died. But I don't want to cry about it. And I don't want to lie when people ask me." I feel helpless, just watching as my child grapples so seriously with himself and his seven-year-old world. He keeps on reciting his line, "dying is part of life," but it's no longer working.

Eli tells Roy he doesn't want to go to the cemetery tomorrow. He's afraid, he says. Afraid of being too sad.

"Everyone will be sad," I tell him. "Many people will cry."

"I don't want to go," he says. "I'm afraid of being more sad than I am already. I don't want that." We decide that he and

Eva can stay back at Leon and Gloria's house with the caterers. They can watch TV like they usually do when we go to visit. This makes them both happy.

Eli's right about being too sad. Burials are brutal, and so is death. It's been a full three years since my mother has died and it hasn't made the reality of death less hard. I see why my mother tried not to look. And what about Gloria's dying of cancer? I think it's the death I fear the most. The stories that Cecile told me about changing her mother's oozing bandages will never go away. When Cecile was dying of cancer, when Eva was only a newborn, I hardly dared to look. Even though I treasured my friendship with Cecile, our many years of monthly dinners together, at the end I never visited her in the hospital when I imagined the devastation must have been the worst. Maybe it's better to die suddenly—to drown in a beautiful place like my mother did, and not have to think about it. I try to stop thinking. It's beginning to seem like the childhood question of whether it's better to be run over by a car or a truck. As if there's a choice to be made.

Danny must have thought a lot about death before he died, about death and about his body. He tested it by cutting his finger first. And before that when he slashed up his T-shirt in front of my mother. And there had been the jacket that Danny had slashed up, too. It was the brown corduroy one that he'd worn in to perfection. Carefully he'd cut out the entire back, and replaced it with patches that he'd sewn together, mostly from scraps of fabric he must have found in my mother's sewing bag. One patch was a piece of once-crisp white cotton with bright blue and turquoise circles, from the curtains in the bedroom Teddy and I once shared in Marblehead.

There was a piece of red printed corduroy with gray emblems that my mother had used for the matching bathrobes she'd made for Teddy and Danny. And there was a square of white and blue checked linen left over from the pleated skirt I had made in home economics class. That skirt had been my greatest sewing accomplishment. I'd even sewn white plastic buckles onto it to make it look like a real kilt. There was a piece of Danny's wool suit. And part of an old tie that had belonged to my father. These were the bits and pieces that held our family together, Danny's final gift to us. His friends told Ted and me that Danny had worn the jacket for at least a month before cutting it into to shreds at the end.

Just before he died, Danny left each of us a personal message, something inscrutable until the meaning became clear later. For me, there had been the phone call about the used clothing store. It was three weeks before he died, the time he came to New York for the Grateful Dead concert and never showed up at my apartment. He called me at work that afternoon, asking for the name of a good used clothing store. "Unique," I'd told him and gave him the address, knowing it was the perfect suggestion. After he died, that phone call about the used clothes replayed in my mind, never to be forgotten. The last time Danny and I really had fun together had been right before Ted's best friend Peter's wedding in Vermont that last Memorial Day weekend before Danny died. We'd all known Peter since childhood and the whole family had been invited. While everyone else was resting or getting ready for the ceremony, Danny and I spent the afternoon trying on old things in a vintage clothing shop in Woodstock. I modeled a pale pink wedding dress that the shop owner told me was once worn on Valentine's Day, as I vaguely imagined what my future might be.

After Danny died, Ted and I searched for explanations. We examined his room in Providence. That's where we found the remains of his destroyed jacket. We sorted through the numerous spiral notebooks teeming with meticulous details about his interpretation of life. Even though we knew they were maniacal, we also thought they were brilliant. Maybe we'd try to get them published, we said. We pored over his calendar, checking to see which appointments he'd made before his death, and whether he'd written down plans for any dates following. Our thirst for information was unquenchable, even though we knew that nothing we could possibly find could help us. We braved ourselves, and went into the restaurant where he'd worked and killed himself. The boss wasn't there, but we sat down at one of the carved wooden tables, just waiting for a while, absorbing the air of the place. We got an appointment with Danny's psychiatrist, who allotted Ted and me a fifty minute time slot. At least he was smart enough not to ask us to pay for it. In the last months of Danny's life, I'd pleaded with him to at least see a therapist. And now I could see that when he'd consented to give it a try, Danny had only found someone else to fool. When Ted and I met the psychiatrist, he didn't say much at all. We managed to pull out of him that he hadn't even known that Danny had a brother or sister. "What did you and Danny talk about?" I asked, my tone I'm sure accusatory, already certain there would be no answers here. He showed no emotion at all, sitting stiffly in his chair across the room from us. Mostly they'd discussed Danny's plans for the future, he told us. We closed his door behind us, more unfulfilled than before.

Fourteen

Eli has just gotten a new short haircut, too short. His head looks like it's been shorn, and has the effect of making his dark eyes look even larger than usual. When he comes into my bedroom from the other side of the apartment, he looks very sad and the whites of his eyes are red, like he's been crying.

"What's wrong?" I ask.

"I don't know," he answers. It's not that easy to get information out of Eli these days, but I persist.

"Does it have to do with Dad?" I ask, knowing that he's just been in the kitchen with Roy.

"No."

"With Gloria?" I ask, even though this seems unlikely. Eli hasn't mentioned Gloria at all lately.

"No," he says again.

Neither of my children seem to be brooders. Eli can be a sensitive soul, but he usually doesn't sit with disappointment or sadness for long. And Eva, while dramatic by nature, moves past her emotional outbursts quickly. "The performance is over now, Eva," Roy often says to her. I count myself lucky to have two children with basically sunny dispositions, but still it can be hard to just sit back and let the odds fall. With my family's history of emotional pitfalls, I'll probably always wonder about how much nature and nurture can really be divided, and where we all reside in that constellation. But down deep, I'm pretty sure we're on a good route.

"Does it have to do with school?" I ask Eli.

"I don't think so."

"With your friends?"

"I don't know. Mom, I'm only telling *you* that I'm sad. No one else."

"Does it have to do with me?" I keep guessing.

"I don't think so."

"Eva?"

"I don't know."

I leave it alone, thinking this is probably one of the countless situations that will make itself known later. But then suddenly, Eli's ready to talk. "It has to do with milk," he blurts out.

"What?" I say. And we both burst into laughter. Eli is doubled over at the nonsense of his words, while I laugh at the absurdity of my worry. "Dad made me drink milk again!" Eli stamps his foot. "If there's one thing I hate, it's milk!"

I breathe in deeply at the beauty and humor of my life. "I'm such a lucky mother," I tell my children repeatedly, even though they probably don't know what I'm talking about. I'm happy for that, too.

~

We're ready to leave for Connecticut to visit Ted and Janet for the Fourth of July weekend. It will be fun to go to the beach together like we did last year. And my father will meet us there. We'll catch him before he leaves next week with Judith on a trip to Italy, Judith's first trip out of the country.

As I turn off the fans and pull down the shades, I stop to pick up the ringing phone. Out of the blue, it's Aunt Anita, my father's sister who lives in Westchester. I can't remember Anita ever calling our apartment before except maybe once to speak to my father when he was visiting. She's talking fast and she's assuming I understand what she's talking about. She is in fact trying to reach my father and she thinks he's here with me. She's talking about "the fall" and "the hospital" and my father calling her that morning and never calling her back again. I piece together that it's Great-Aunt Sylvia that's causing the alarm. Aunt Sylvia is now ninety-seven and she's been feuding with Aunt Anita for decades. For years, Anita catered to Sylvia's whims, dutifully fulfilling her role as beleaguered niece, until Sylvia's complete disrespect became too insufferable even for Anita. More recently my father has taken on the job of tending to Aunt Sylvia, albeit from 200 miles away in Boston. "I'm giving all my money to Israel when I die!" is Sylvia's ongoing threat, although we all doubt there can really be much left from the dockworker's pension that her husband left her forty years ago.

On the topic of Aunt Sylvia, I side with my mother, who charged Sylvia with being ridiculously self-centered, even if she was an old woman. Twenty years ago at my grandmother's funeral, I'd been shocked by Sylvia's words. "I have no tears to shed!" she shouted as they lowered the body of her older, prettier, and more gracious sister into the grave. For a few years when I first moved to New York, I tried to make a tradition of taking Great-Aunt Sylvia to lunch at B. Altman's every few months, thinking I was being deferential to this old aunt who lived on her own. But eventually, especially when she sent Ted the check for $1,000 after Danny died and ignored me completely, I gave up on being nice.

My father likes to think that family is important, so he takes his job of taking care of Sylvia seriously. He reports regularly to Ted and me on Sylvia's status, even though we don't care very much. Lately, he's told us, Sylvia's housekeeping and her appearance have become disorderly. And she refuses to allow the social worker to enter her apartment, convinced that she's been tampering with her checkbook. Most recently even my father has been thought to be a threat, and she's asked him to return the key to her apartment. But until Anita's phone call I hadn't heard anything about Sylvia being taken to the hospital.

"He had to call 911," Aunt Anita is saying, "when Sylvia's neighbor reported that Sylvia hadn't answered her phone for three days." The ambulance driver had to break down Sylvia's locked door, and he found her lying unconscious on the floor. Then she ended up at Einstein Hospital in the Bronx, where they said she had a broken hip. "But that was a few days ago," says Anita. Hadn't my father mentioned it? "Sylvia is now refusing to have hip surgery. That's why Joel drove down—to take care of things," she says. "They were going to send her back to her apartment on her own, if she didn't agree to the surgery." Anita had been waiting all day by the phone for my father's call from the hospital, but he'd never called. Where was he? "I don't know what to say," I tell her. "I'll find out more. I'll call him once I get to Ted's. And then I'll call you." It sounds tumultuous and irresponsible even for my father, but not impossible either.

When we arrive at Ted's house, the first thing I do is call my father. "Just walked in the door, Annie," he says, his voice cheerful. When I ask him about Aunt Sylvia, he tells me it's been a long haul for one day, but he's visited Sylvia in the hospital and successfully convinced her to have the operation on her hip, and now he's made it back to Andover. He'll see us at the beach tomorrow, he says. And two days later, he says with satisfaction, he and Judith will be on their way to Italy.

"You'd better call Anita," I tell him. "She's been waiting all day to hear from you."

"Right," he says. "I'll do that."

"Dad, why didn't you say anything to Ted or me about Aunt Sylvia?" I ask him.

"She was fine," he says. "911 took care of getting her to the hospital. It was only when she refused the operation that she got into trouble. And that only just happened today. Now everything's taken care of."

I cringe at the thought of my father as caretaker. Yet he *is* my father, the one who I always believed wanted to take care of me when my mother couldn't come through.

The next morning we all convene at the beach on the Fourth of July, as planned. My father arrives last, reporting that he's found a great parking spot in the grocery store lot. He spreads out his towel and goes to join the grandchildren who have already begun to build a sandcastle. The kids are already hungry so Ted and I go to the snack bar to get sandwiches. When we return, my father is folding up his towel and preparing to leave. "You're going now?" I ask. "You just got here."

"I need to leave," he tells me. "I told Judith I'd help her with tonight's dinner. You know, we invited over a couple who's just returned from Italy and who may have some interesting tips," he says. "Besides, I may be parked illegally and I don't want to get a ticket."

"But we arranged this day at the beach a month ago," I start to berate him. But I stop myself from going on, from pointing out that it was because he wanted to spend time with the grandchildren that we'd planned the trip to begin with. His logic has always been his own, and I know he loves his grandchildren. Just like he believes he's doing a good job taking care of Aunt Sylvia. "Bye, Dad," I say. "Have a good dinner tonight."

The next day when I call him to say goodbye again, he's in excellent spirits. "It's a good thing I left yesterday when I did," he tells me. "The patrol car was just coming into the grocery store parking lot to give tickets to the illegally parked cars." He'd managed to park the car in the lot and not get a ticket.

Communicating with my father has always required taking one step back. His actions don't necessarily mesh with what his intentions seem to be. And the fact is, that's demanding. His brand of being a father requires a kind of care in return. If I can remember to pay attention to that, maybe I can finally be an adult with him. I can only hope that my own children will always feel my love clearly.

Fifteen

This year we're staying a week longer in Deer Isle—five whole weeks. We had to give up our round house because the owner wouldn't rent for that long. But the new place is set right on the harbor in Stonington and from the photos, it looks ideal. We'll have a different post office and a different dump this year—significant changes in our simple island existence.

Sitting on top of a hill, the redone farmhouse really does look picture perfect. And once we get inside and the door slams behind us, we can see that everything is very clean and tidy. "It's tight," as Roy puts it. The owner had rebuilt it as a retirement home, but when his wife died suddenly last fall, he decided to rent it out instead, and stay in his other house up the road. The kids run upstairs ahead of us. The large master bedroom has a spectacular view of the harbor. And the sheets and blankets are all brand new. But when I see the kids' room, I start to worry. It was supposed to have twin beds, not a double. How will Eli and Eva ever cooperate enough to share one bed? The third bedroom is small with two insubstantial cots that don't look very inviting. And my father and Leon are supposed to visit the week after next. There's no deck, not even a porch. And there are no screens on the windows, as if they're not meant to be opened. We've left our city world for the outdoors of Deer Isle, and that's not what's here in this sealed off house.

I try not to be disappointed as I forage through the kitchen cabinets, to see what kinds of pots and pans there are. The owner's wife must have been a baker because there are plenty of muffin tins and measuring cups. The kitchen table, I notice, is made of nice wood, but it's meant to seat exactly four, perfect for a retired couple, but not for us. My mind goes to long summer dinners laughing with guests, and my heart drops a little more. We've made a mistake. "We liked the other house better!" the kids shout out. "Why can't we go back there?"

Roy finds some extra leaves to expand the table, and we find some additional dining room chairs scattered around the house. "Let's go to get something to eat," he says. "In the morning, we'll go to the hardware store to find some screens for the windows." Roy's right, after the nine-hour drive, we're too exhausted to do anything about the house now. We go out to pick up some milk and orange juice for the morning, and luckily the pizza restaurant is still open for dinner.

In the morning we discover the benefits of the easy ten minute walk into town. There's a market, the post office, and a homemade ice cream place. The owner of the house lends us a big log table that he doesn't use. He tows it down the road for us, so we can have lunch outside. Eli and Eva befriend the eleven-year-old girl who lives next door. Eva loves the neighbor's long blond hair, and she's happy to play catch with Eli, too. Maybe we'll have an idyllic month in Maine after all. As

Roy and I unpack, Eli and Eva and the neighbor are already setting up a croquet course on the lawn.

The kids are eager to get to the Lily Pond, and once the day gets warm enough, we're on our way. I leave Eli, Eva, and Roy on the banks of the pond. Slowly I wade in up to my waist before I begin to swim. This first swim in the pond is a big deal, after the disquiet that marked the end of last summer when the man drowned. For the first couple of minutes, I keep my head above the surface. Once I dare to submerge my head, the bubbles make a thundering sound when I breathe. I can feel my heart beating. I pass my old landmarks—the rounded gray rock and the spotted, pointy one. When I get to the swinging rope, still hanging there from years past, I turn back. I'll wait until next time to go all the way to the big yellow rock on the right. It hasn't been a relaxing swim, but I've done it. I breathe in the Maine air.

Roy leaves for New York, the kids start camp, and I begin to swim daily as though I'm on some kind of a mission. Each swim seems to get progressively longer and better. Yesterday was pure delight, the air warm and calm.

Today it's so beautiful I decide to get to the pond a little early, leaving extra time for an even longer swim before I have to pick up the kids at camp. Maybe I'll even make it all the way to the other side. No matter what, I want to swim until I'm really ready to turn back. Once I'm out in the middle of the pond, it's breezier than I'd expected. But still it's lovely. I survey the beauty of the trees and rocks along the shore. It's familiar now, but as always strikingly beautiful. Then suddenly, with no warning, there's another swimmer, stroking strongly and moving diagonally across the pond, and I can see that it's a matter of only a couple of minutes until we intersect. I can't figure out where he's come from. I definitely did not see him enter from the round gray rock on the left, or further out by the swinging rope.

As we approach one another, I quickly glance around and see that there's no one else in the water. I try to remain cheerful and give the usual nod hello between strokes, but the man does not respond to my gesture. He's now close enough for me to get a fairly good look at his face, and I can see that the top of his forehead is a little caved in. I keep on swimming and try casually to switch from my usual breaststroke to the sidestroke, so I can keep an eye on him. I wish him back to land, although I still can't figure out where he came from, or his destination point.

I'll turn back, I tell myself. If something is going to happen to me, it's better to be closer to the beach where other people might see me. I switch back to breaststroke, so I can swim faster, but mostly I keep my face above water, to keep track of the man. Finally I see him get out of the pond. He climbs onto the round gray rock, and I'm pretty sure he's looking right at me. He slowly puts on long pants, a belt and shoes, not the usual pond attire, and walks off into the woods, out of sight at last. Still I'm eager to get back, increasing my speed and sputtering in the now choppy water. When I get to my towel, I have plenty of time. But I put on my shorts right away and drive over to the camp, and wait for the kids in the parking lot.

That night, I dream that I see the man in town. His head looks less bent in than it did in the pond. And this time, he raises his eyebrow at me, like he's saying hello.

It's a hot and steamy day, not at all like Maine. Eli's been up for most of the night with a stomach bug, so he's staying home from camp today with me. Between the heat and Eli's fever, I haven't slept much either. We play cards and doze off. Eli wakes up from a nap, and on the table next to him he sees an old *New York Times* that hasn't been thrown out yet. He snatches it, thinking he'll find the Yankees' score. "You won't find it there," I say. "It's last Sunday's paper." Then I count the days since last Sunday, trying to figure out today's date. It's Danny's birthday, I realize. That's probably why Ted called me earlier this morning to say hello.

"It's August ninth," I say aloud. "Danny's birthday."

"Danny was your brother." Eli has by now become familiar with this fact. It's part of the information I've slowly been parceling out to him over time. "He was twenty-two when he died," he says with authority. And I nod back.

"How did he die?" Eli asks. We've never gotten this far before. Groggy from the heat, I'm dimly aware that he's just asked me the question I'd be waiting to answer for his whole life. And now all of a sudden, it's my turn to tell him.

"Well, something went wrong with his brain," I hear myself say. This is real. No longer the words I'd rehearsed. "He had a kind of sickness in his mind," I tell Eli. "He actually killed himself. It's a very, very unusual thing," I tell him slowly, trying to somehow protect him. "It will probably never happen to anyone you know." I wonder whether my words can possibly make any sense.

"What did he do?" Eli is clearly engaged. He wants to know more. "How did he kill himself? Was it with a gun?" Of course this is a predictable part of the conversation. Eli wants details, but for some reason I hadn't anticipated that.

"No, with a knife," I hear myself say. "He stabbed himself."

"In the heart?" asks Eli.

"Well, sort of near the heart." I know I must be truthful despite my aversion to what I'm saying. "It was really a very, very weird and unusual thing," I repeat. "His brain was not working right when it happened. It was a type of sickness."

"If he hadn't done that, would he have died anyway?" Already Eli is far beyond my simple explanation, asking the very question I have asked myself infinite times.

"He might have," I answer. "Or he might have just been very sick for the rest of his life. Like I said, his brain wasn't working right."

"Was he sick for a long time?"

"Well, sort of yes. On and off for a couple of years. But before those years he was a really wonderful brother. Forty-one years ago, when Danny was born, I was six years old. He was my adorable baby brother. And he grew into a very funny and remarkable person, a wonderful friend. I loved him very much."

"I wish Danny were still alive," says Eli. "I wish I knew him."

"Me, too," I say. "I think a lot about how much he would have loved you and Eva, and how much you would have loved him."

"He would be my uncle," Eli says.

"He's still your uncle," I say.

"Will that ever happen to me? What happened to Danny?" asks Eli.

He's asking me exactly what I want him to know. "Never," I say adamantly. "That would be impossible."

I try to explain that what happened to Danny happened because his brain made him be in a lot of pain. And what he did made everyone else in a lot of pain, too. "It was the sad-dest I've ever been in my whole life," I tell him. I feel my tears coming, but I don't let myself cry. I leave out how scared I was, and how many years it's taken me to separate myself from the violence and the misery of it, how it's a wound that will never go away completely.

"I'd never do that," says Eli.

"I know."

Eli stares hard at me. He now knows something very new and different, and he'll have a lifetime to process it, and to think of more questions. This conversation had to happen.

"We can talk about this more some other time," I say as we return to the game of Go Fish we'd begun before his nap. "When you get older."

≈

Roy returns to us for the last weeks of August. We've adjusted to our house on the harbor. It's noisy in the early hours of the morning when the lobster boats go out, still not the ideal spot we imagined. But we like it here. The kids finish camp, and spend the days running outdoors and swimming. I've taken any number of beautiful swims myself. Sometimes I've made it just short of the other end of the pond. But that no longer seems particularly essential.

Roy's even found out about a beautiful house that may be available next summer. It's set in a lovely cove, and it's right up against the water. From the inside when you look out, the ocean reflects through the old glass window panes, like a dream. If I've ever had a dream of a summer house in Maine, maybe it's this.

By the end of the month, I know it's been a lovely summer. The kids have been happy and free. Eli has seen hummingbirds and a great blue heron, and Eva has made necklaces out of shells. With weather unusually warm for these regions, the days have been long, lasting right through into the fading light of the evening on the water. We've discovered new beaches and trails, and we've wallowed in old haunts.

Knowing how sad I'll be to leave this place for the fall, I tread slowly into the Lily Pond for my last swim in the pond this year. So much has changed this summer. Over the past Augusts, and past years, I've labored so hard to find the way to grieve for my mother and at last I've come to know that it's my grief for Danny that holds that key. I'll never reconcile with the reality that Danny had to die, but I think I can accept the mystery of it, that I'll never know for sure whether it could have been different. Danny's death has now become part of my family legacy. In all of its havoc and violence, I've passed the fact of it along to Eli, not as a secret to be hidden, but as something to know and to live with. My mother no longer holds the knot of Danny, and of all the deaths before his. And with this I am now free to feel her imprinted in my mind, just as she was—strong, determined, and fearful—the mother I knew, the mother I longed for.

I absorb the calm and the beauty of the pond as though I might be able to store it for the year ahead. Once we're back at home, I'll find the time to tell my children that their grandmother died swimming on the other side of the world. Stroking through the fresh, cool water, watching the movement of the ripples all around, I swim my final laps of the season.

Biographical Note

Anne Edelstein has worked in the book publishing business for over twenty-five years, as an editor and then as a literary agent in New York City, where she lives with her family. This is her first book.